Adventures in the Redwoods

HARRIETT E. WEAVER

 Chronicle Books

DEDICATION
To you—the Adventurer

Previous Books by Harriett E. Weaver:
There Stand the Giants
Frosty, A Raccoon to Remember
Bahamas, A Bull to Remember

Printed in the United States of America
ISBN 0-87701-060-9
Library of Congress Catalog Card Number: 75-3912

Acknowledgements

Rarely does a book of this kind spring full blown and complete in every respect from the brain and efforts of one person. This one certainly didn't. It is a composite of what I have read and learned and seen over many years of close association with redwood country and its people, both as a park ranger and as a long-time writer and teacher of California—the geography, geology, history, natural resources, industry, where-to-go and what-to-see. Even so, a book could not have evolved without the many gracious offers of resources and assistance; the packets of current data and excellent photographs placed at my disposal. Such support is what makes a book go, and sets it as factually correct as is possible in the quick-change life we are living. Well wishes, too, add much to the zest of producing something of interest and value.

I hope *Adventures in the Redwoods* can serve as a useful companion to anyone with the yen to explore tall forests of giant trees and who has the gasoline to do it with. If so, and whether you are afoot or horseback or aboard a bike or a bus or in your own car, I'd like you to know that the following agencies and individuals had a hand in your enjoyment. To them and for this I am deeply grateful.

American Forests Magazine - James B. Craig, Editor.

California Redwood Association - Pamela Allsebrook, Public Relations and Information.

California Western Railroad (The Skunk) - R. A. Regalia, General Manager.

Chamber of Commerce, Santa Rosa, California - Thomas Cox, Executive Director.

Coastal Parks Association, Inc. - Pt. Reyes National Seashore, Muir Woods National Monument, Redwood National Park - Thomas G. Vaughan, Executive Secretary.

Earl P. Hanson, Chief, Division of Beaches and Parks, retired.

Lane Publishing Company, Menlo Park, Dave Clark, Executive Editor of Sunset Books.

Masonite Corporation.

National Park Service - James Sleznick Jr., Chief of Visitor Service and Public Information, Yosemite National Park. Larry Rose, Supervisory Park Ranger, Klamath Ranger Station. James W. Howell, Management Assistant, Sequoia and Kings Canyon National Parks.

Redwood Empire Association - Norma Flanery, Publicity.

Redwood Region Conservation Council - Bud Good, Information Officer.
Rellim Redwood Company - Richard L. Brown, Chief Forester.
Save-the-Redwood League - Newton B. Drury, President.
Sempervirens Fund - "Tony" Look, Executive Vice-President.
State Department of Conservation - Raymond R. Higgins, Information Officer.
State Department of Parks and Recreation - Brenda Boswell, Editor of News and Views.
State Division of Forestry - Gerald E. Newton, Assistant Director of Public Affairs.
University of California, College of Natural Resources - Rudolf F. Grah, Chairman.
Also numerous park rangers, lumbermen, and other citizens of redwood country.

Photographic Credits

Contents

6   Adventures in the Redwoods

California's
Giant Trees

California's giant redwoods are renowned every-
where on earth, and rightfully so. Where else but in the coastal forests
can you stand in a shadowy world of stillness and tranquillity and let
your gaze wander up a living shaft to a canopy of green foliage often
hidden by clouds and drifting fog? Where else but in the high mountains a hundred miles inland from there must twenty to thirty people
have to clasp hands before they can encircle a red trunk massive
enough to plug up a city street?

Of three known types of redwoods, two grow in California and
one of them lops over a bit into Oregon. That redwood, the tall coastal
tree, inhabits nine counties along the sea and is scientifically classified
as *Sequoia sempervirens* or Coast redwoods—or just plain redwoods for
short. The bulky Sierra redwood, found in six Sierra Nevada counties,
is classified *Sequoiadendron giganteum*—too much of a mouthful to be
bandied about lightly. We call it the Sequoia or Big Tree. And so it
shall be in this book.

To visit the third member of the relationship, the *Metasequoia*
(new sequoia) or Dawn redwood, you would have to trudge into remote China. Anyway, since this redwood rises a mere hundred feet, is
bare-stemmed in winter, and was thought to have been extinct for
twenty million years, it wouldn't intrigue you like California's own
except as a living fossil, which it truly is.

The story of the giant redwood goes back into antiquity a
hundred million years to a time when much of the planet was covered
with warm seas, when some of its creatures were deserting water for
dry land and monstrous reptiles dominated all living things. Nowhere
as yet were there any broadleaf trees or flowering plants, but towering
above the ungainly dinosaurs were conifers so enormous that they
dwarfed the mightiest of prehistoric beasts. It was of such a time and
place that the redwoods' fight for survival began.

With the passing of long epochs, earthquakes buckled and
shifted entire continents and ocean basins. Volcanoes spewed lava over
vast areas. The sun scorched and withered, and dried up the surface

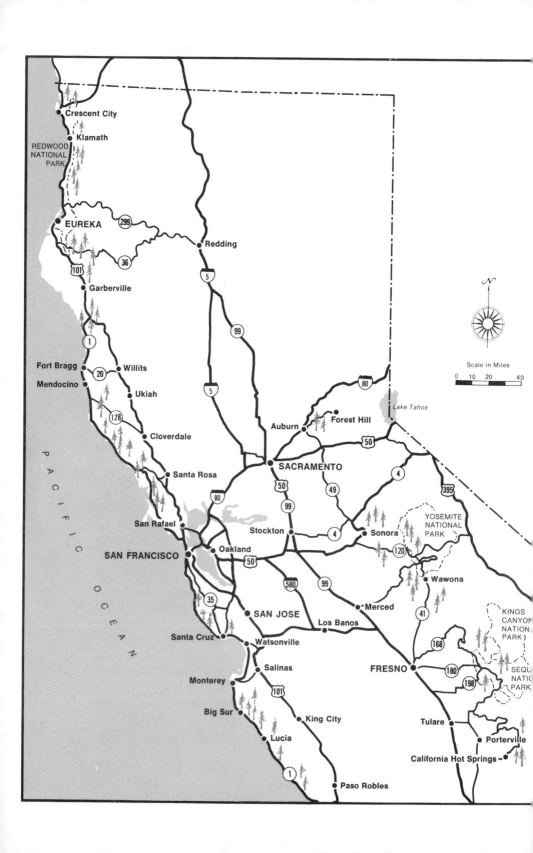

waters. Unable to cope with such cataclysms, the dinosaurs and their kind vanished from the scene, but the big trees that had fed and sheltered them somehow carried forward their own thread of life. And scarcely changing form, this thread has endured through the ages; down through thousands and thousands of centuries of mountain building and extremes of climate.

About 60 million years ago, predecessors of the big redwoods we know today flourished over much of the Northern Hemisphere. Their fossil remains have been discovered among the bones and footprints of dinosaurs, in England, Switzerland, Norway, France, Germany, Austria, Japan, Central Asia, and parts of the United States. It boggles the mind to contemplate how their seeds, together with the migrating animals, crossed the land connection between Siberia and Alaska. On Saint Lawrence Island in the Bering Sea, where now no trees at all can grow, fossil evidence shows that both redwoods and their present companions, the oaks, alders, and maples once existed there. At the same time, Greenland was living up to its name, hosting a luxurious growth. This was before extensive land uplift changed the tropical climate, for even though the Appalachians were then hills thousands of years old, and the Sierra Nevada was forming, the Andes, Alps, Himalayas, and Rockies had not yet risen.

The redwoods, however, were not destined to occupy all their original wide-ranging domain. A million or two years ago advancing ice sheets crowded them into a last stand in California and Southwest Oregon. Along the coast, the retreating glaciers left behind a fairly continuous belt of redwoods about 500 miles long ranging today from below Big Sur, south of Monterey, to a few miles above the California-Oregon border. Always just out of reach of the wind-blown spray, the trees inhabit sheltered, well-watered places of rich soil as far inland as the fog drifts—20 miles or more—and up the Coast Range mountainsides to about 3000 feet—or until good soil, sufficient moisture and suitable slopes give out. Their forests are vast, dark, dense, and understandably lush with an infinite variety of underbrush because of the 80 to 140-inch annual rainfall. Thus, the groves of really magnificent giants stand on riverside flats, where winter floods supplement the lifegiving downpour and provide layers of nutritious sediment as well. And when the winter rains finally wind up for the year, usually in April, often in May, wet summer fogs hover over the forests and slow the sun's evaporation of precious moisture.

The sequoias do not form a continuous band as do the coast redwoods, although they probably did at one time. During the Ice Age, starting about a million years ago, glacial rivers slid down the

Ancient of Ancients

UNTIL THIRTY YEARS AGO, NO botanist would have dreamed of finding a living metasequoia—or Dawn redwood—any more than he would have expected to meet a dinosaur lumbering through our forests. Yet one of our scientists did see such trees.

In 1948 Dr. Ralph W. Chaney, distinguished paleobotanist and professor at the University of California, received word that Chinese forester Tsany Wang had seen what appeared to be living metasequoias in the protected ravines of Szechuan and Hipeh provinces in interior China more than 100 miles northeast of Chunking. Because Dr. Chaney had long known that nowhere had

Dawn redwood fossils appeared in rocks of the last 20,000,000 years, he was understandably skeptical. Still, his curiosity was aroused and he flew to China to see for himself.

Upon reaching Wan Hsien on the Yangtse River, Dr. Chaney accompanied by Dr. Milton Silverman, Science writer for the San Francisco *Chronicle*, and a party of Chinese began a hazardous, rain-drenched trek over precarious passes obscured by clouds, and through jungles infested with bandits, until they came at last to a winding valley. In it was a tiny settlement, some rice paddies, and a small temple. Beside this temple stood a tall

mountainsides from the ice fields that capped the Sierra and quarried out deep gashes such as Yosemite Valley and Kings Canyon. This left the Big Trees standing in some 70 separate groves, most of them isolated from one another. Today there are probably no more than 20,000 sequoias remaining, although they are anything but a dying race of trees as you will agree when you see all the young ones on their way to becoming giants.

The Big Trees prefer the higher, rarer atmosphere of the Sierra's western slope between 4500 and 8000-feet elevation. They range from west of Lake Tahoe south 250 miles to southern Tulare County. In the Sierra, showers fall occasionally in the warm summers, and deep snows remain throughout the long cold winters. Because of such extreme conditions, there is far less underbrush than along the coast. The forest is open and sunny, highlighting the cinnamon-red grandeur of the mightiest trees on earth.

The coast redwoods seem to meld into an atmosphere of reverence akin to that found in a great cathedral—only this cathedral is not of stone but of living walls, softly mauve. Its ceiling is not of hand-carved rafters but of open sky; its windows not of stained glass but of

tree 98 feet high and 64 inches through above the base flare. Several more grew nearby. Farther on, in Hupeh Province, they came to a hundred or so large trees scattered in small groves across the mountain slopes, along the paddies, and back into the canyons. The few villagers called them water pines because of requiring so much moisture—which of course they did because they actually were redwoods—living metasequoias.

And as Dr. Chaney and Dr. Silverman described the incredible scene: "The valley was like North America looked 30,000,000 years ago before the creation of the Cascade Range, before the Sierra Nevada, Rockies, and Appalachians rose to their present grandeur. When most of our West Coast was still under the Pacific."

There in the valley, as in California's redwood country today, the summers are warm, the winters mild and wet. In this remote spot, the last of the world's Dawn redwoods had found refuge where great protective ranges had pushed up a mile high all around, providing for the living fossils a veritable Shangra-la.

During the 80,000,000 years the redwoods had struggled to perpetuate their kind by migrating south ahead of the advancing ice-sheets, all were thought to have been lost except the two de-

lacy foliage high above, through which the sun filters in golden shafts.

A community of Big Trees, on the other hand, creates an entirely different aura. Here you are sure to be awed by the immense grandeur and indestructibility of individual sequoias, partly because of the starkness of their tremendous trunks. Like Doric columns they rise almost without taper for the first hundred or more feet to the first limb, itself as large and sometimes as long as the conifers you camp under in lesser forests.

In age, the coast redwoods do not compare with the Big Trees. By actual ring count, the oldest known Coast redwood has lived 2200 years. It is only 12 feet in diameter, not nearly as large as countless others much younger that have grown up under more favorable conditions. It was felled in 1934 in the Avenue of the Giants, Humboldt County, in a very dense forest, so it never did attain the height and bulk it might have, had abundant sunlight been available. Most Coast redwoods measure 10 to 12 feet in diameter, some up to 18 or more feet and are as much as 60 feet around. One of the largest known, the Santa Clara Tree in Big Basin Redwoods State Park, measures 17 feet 9 inches at breast height (4½ feet above the ground and root swell) and

(continued from p. 11)

scendents in California because only fossil remnants of them had ever been found. How anything living could have come so close to extinction and still survive is one of the fantastic mysteries of life on earth.

Growing among these miracles stands a mixture of ancient oaks, birch, sweet gum, chestnut, beech, and Katsura—the same trees that together with the redwoods had once sheltered the dinosaurs, and which now appear nowhere else in the same association.

Also among them is a profusion of azalea, rhododendron, wild iris, berries, and yew trees—the close associates of redwoods today.

Dr. Chaney flew back to the University of California bringing several young seedlings, surely the most precious botannical specimens in the nation. These were planted at Berkeley, and because of them, hundreds more are now flourishing from Alaska to Panama, wherever there is a temperate, moist environment. At Big Basin, Henry Cowell Redwoods, and Prairie Creek Redwoods state parks you will find specimen trees.

Back in China a Metasequoia Conservation Committee has been formed, which seeks to preserve its groves of living fossils, the ancient metasequoia, only ones of their kind on earth.

---

55 feet in circumference. Rising straight and impressive, the Santa Clara tapers so little that at 100 feet it is still 40 feet around—not massive like some of the monstrous Big Trees in the Sierra, but nevertheless a giant to behold among the slenderer coast trees.

Only comparisons familiar to the human scope of experience can bring into focus the incredible dimensions of the Big Trees, such as the General Sherman in Sequoia National Park. Its first limb, 130 feet above the ground, is as big through as some professional basketball players are tall—almost 7 feet. A grammar school boy, racing from one base to another, would be running the distance through the General—somewhat more than 33 feet. And the whopper probably weights 2½ million pounds, the weight of 80 freight locomotives or about 600 pickup trucks.

The age of the General can only be estimated, but botanists believe the giant to be over 3500 years. If such be the case, it would already have seen more than 1500 summers and winters the night the star appeared over Bethlehem and more than 3000 by the time Columbus discovered America. Some of the sequoias are thought to be approaching 4000 years—not quite as ancient as the bristlecone pines

Rain Forest: Mist hovers around the great redwood forests of Northern California, providing continuous and vital moisture during the unusually rainless summer and autumn months.

Youngsters on a Saturday picnic at Big Basin try to encircle the Santa Clara Tree.

Petrified Forest

NOT ALL OF CALIFORNIA'S RED-woods are alive, however. Some are more than dead. These, discovered in 1871, had been transformed into stone. Far, far in the ancient past a nearby mountain blew its top, hurled the giants to earth, all pointed away from the violence that leveled them, then covered them with volcanic waste.

This was Mt. St. Helena in Sonoma County those hundreds of centuries ago. Today the mountain slumbers peacefully, watching over a valley of vineyards, although around it remain vestiges of long ago fires—mud holes, fumeroles, geysers, hot mineral springs—and a Petrified Forest.

Over a period of years the trees were excavated, not as stumps and fragments but as entire redwood trunks, some found as deep as 90 feet in the earth. Their textures and story has been perfectly preserved even to the petrified worms embedded in the wood and growth rings that tell the ages of the trees down to the day of their destruction. You can visit them in a little private park five miles west of Calistoga on the Santa Rosa road. Among them is The Queen of the Forest, 80 feet long and 12 feet in diameter and The Monarch, 126 feet long and 8 feet through. Every year hundreds of visitors are attracted to this unique melding of geologic forces and living tissue.

---

in the White Mountains of eastern California, but big and old and healthy enough to be a prime botanical wonder of the world.

Despite the General's hoary age, it rises only 272 feet, just about par for sequoias. This is amazing when compared with much younger coast redwoods, most of which sweep the clouds at well over 200 feet, the height of a 20-story building.

For years, the 364-foot Founders Tree at Dyerville Flats in the Redwood Empire topped all living things. Then a storm whacked off the tip. A few years later, some towering 368-foot trees were discovered on private lands in an area on Redwood Creek east of Orick, now a part of the Redwood National Park. The new champions may in turn be challenged anytime some intrepid explorer finds a taller tree, or if lightning bolts and hurricane-force winds tear off their lofty crowns, or if falling neighbors expose a tree to full sunlight, releasing it to head for the open sky at 3 feet a year.

Together, the coastal giants form a skyscraping forest. As they grow older and rise higher and higher, and after their crowns have merged into a dark canopy that permits almost no passage of sunlight,

The Indian Arrow Tree

REDWOOD COUNTRY HAS MANY special trees, but just east of Korbel in Humboldt County is a *special* special giant, known as the Indian Arrow Tree, now a California Registered Landmark.

Legend has it that in some remote time the upland Indians offended the Great Spirit, who punished them with a drought. Because they then began to starve and together with the forest animals were forced into the lowlands for food and water, the Mad River Indians resented their intrusion with a full scale fight. To stop the warring, the Great Spirit promised rain if the two chiefs would sit in peace beside a certain tree. Then, to perpetually honor this tree as the site of their peace-making, the Great Spirit decreed that whoever passed it thereafter was to shoot an arrow into its trunk. The squaws were to push a green bough into its bark as high as they could reach.

For countless years the Indians paid homage in this manner until at last, by the 1880's, the redwood was a fuzz stick of arrows and green boughs 60 feet up the trunk. Finally someone set it afire. Only a few of the highest arrows escaped the flames.

Today, all that remains of the Indian Arrow Tree is an old redwood snag. Surrounded by a new generation of vigorous youngsters, it stands proudly, a weathered monument to the days before the coming of white men. Gone are the arrows, of course, but for years arrowheads could be found around its gnarled surface roots.

---

they drop their lower limbs, laying bare their trunks a long way up.

The volume of board footage contained in such trees is difficult to grasp. For our imaginations to be stirred, we have to compare the immense timber volume with familiar things. Men with slide rules and an eye for construction can tell that twenty 5-room cottages could be built from the Santa Clara Tree (Heaven forbid), or, from even larger redwoods, a school of a hundred class rooms with enough left over for an auditorium. In like terms, the General Sherman could be spoken of as forty 5-room cottages, or, as has been stated by park naturalists, a crate large enough to house the Queen Mary.

One might imagine that anything as tall and slender as a coast redwood must surely be anchored near the center of the earth. Not so. Not so the sequoia either. Supporting all that spectacular bulk and weight is a remarkable balance, poised precariously on a pocket of roots so shallow as to defy belief. The root pad extends downward only 6 or 8 feet, although the network of small feeder roots may spread over several acres. The coast redwoods root themselves only 4 to 6 feet

The General Sherman is the giant of giants—102
feet in circumference and containing about 600,000
board feet of straight-grained wood.

*The massive upended root system of one of
Mariposa Grove's fallen giants provides a
challenge for young vacationers.*

down, and their feeder roots, some hair-fine and just inches beneath
the forest floor litter, reach out only one or two hundred feet, entwin-
ing with the roots of their neighbors. Neither type of redwood has a
taproot to ram its way far below and act as a groundgripper, holding the
columns solidly erect through the centuries. Nothing continues to bur-
row deeper and deeper into the mother soil as the trees rise higher and
higher above it. The only really strong anchorage both giants have is
surface roots. Like great claws they clutch the ground at the base. But
even so, these sometimes fail to save a tall willowy redwood from
toppling in the furious winds off the sea that whip the tree tops back
and forth. Even when the roots hold, the trunks creak and groan, and
huge limbs crash to the ground. These are called "Widowmakers" by
rangers and their wives for a reason easy to guess.

Along with such storms, erosion is the redwoods' worst natural
enemy. Every year many fall as floodwaters tear away the soil around
their roots and slipping mountainsides bulldoze them over. Giants

come crashing down, and when they do, the earth shakes. Even the largest of trees are carried away by the water, some clear to the sea, where they litter the beaches.

Others may not drop completely but simply lean, possibly because a section of their root systems has been killed by fire, or some of their neighbors, in falling, have forced them off kilter. To save themselves, the leaners ingeniously redistribute the weight of their trunks by widening the growth rings on the weak side while narrowing and sometimes discontinuing them on the opposite side, thereby building a buttress of wood. The longer the giant stands, the larger and sturdier the buttress becomes, forming what is known as a flatiron tree. With this support, it may survive longer than redwoods that have always stood straight and undisturbed.

The Big Trees rely on a different procedure. When one of them is thrown off plumb, it begins to send out huge limbs away from the lean, arms stretching out and up in an effort to restore balance very much the same as we do while trying to walk a narrow beam.

After you see lightning zigzag across the sky or watch on television flames roaring through thousands of acres of forestlands, you may wonder why the long-lived redwoods are not consumed like all the other trees. The answer is that the great trees are protected by multiple defenses that guard them against fire, disease, and decay.

Their first line of defense against fire is a soft pithy bark—on the coast redwoods a foot or less thick, on the sequoias up to 3 feet through, and so asbestos-like as to be virtually fireproof.

The bark contains no pitch or resin, the sticky substance that causes trees like pines and firs to flare up in such a hurry. In addition, the wood beneath the bark contains a great deal of water, which slows burning even when a blaze manages to gain entrance through a break in the bark. The great blackened caverns, so often found in the base of big old giants, were probably the work of not one but a series of holocausts over a long period of time. Such wildfires usually destroy the rest of the forest, including young redwoods that have not yet had time to mature and develop thick hides.

Not only does the bark save the trees from fire; it protects them against heat and cold as well. Even should the interior be blazing fiercely, the bark would still be cool to the touch.

Sometimes lightning plays havoc with the treetops, setting crown fires and shattering limbs, but the electricity will not be carried downward via the bark because it is a nonconductor. Attempts to force as much as 5000 volts through it have failed. Small wonder that redwood bark is considered an excellent insulating material.

In any forest, falling trees usually strike and injure others. After such an occurrence or a fire, a redwood's "growing" part gets busy and does some healing work. This is the thin cambium layer just beneath the bark that widens the tree by one ring each year. Eventually, it 'forms a new skin that closes the wound, much as human flesh responds to a similar need. Other trees aren't long-lived enough to heal their injuries; but a giant has all the time in the world—with luck, many centuries. And so effective can its coverup be that no one would ever suspect that there is a great charred hole sealed off from view inside that huge trunk. In time, scar tissue and even outer bark will have completely obliterated all trace. Only after the giant is down and a cross-section taken, will the truth be discovered.

Some living giants, fire-hollowed clear out the top, invite you to look up at the sky through their center. The Chimney Tree in Big Basin Redwoods State Park and the Telescope Tree in the Mariposa Grove, Yosemite, are two of the best known.

The burned-out heartwood is the giants' first and oldest growth and is dead tissue, so its loss is not a devastating one. What's important is the living tissue, the cream-colored sapwood surrounding it that conducts water and minerals from the roots up to the leaves, where they are converted into food, and the inner bark that carries nutrients downward to supply the whole tree. After a fire, if enough of the sapwood remains in contact with the earth to pull sufficient moisture as high as the crown, the vigorous and healthy foliage and cones will be ample evidence of continuing life. If not, the top may die. Most of the "spiketops" seen on the forest skyline are the result of fire damage; the rest have been caused by lightning strikes and wind damage.

In addition to the thick, fire-resistant bark, the trees are further protected by special chemicals—principally tannin. You can see it in the vivid coloring of both bark and heartwood and sometimes as a dark stain flowing over raw broken surfaces, creosoting them against the ravages of time and the invasion of insects and disease, which occurs when a tree fractures in crashing to the ground and is left there.

Almost all fallen trees decay rather rapidly—but not redwoods. Thanks to their tannin, even giants that have lain partially buried for centuries are in good enough condition to be hauled away to the mill and sawed into lumber, the same as standing trees.

Redwoods are sometimes attacked by insects and fungi but almost never damaged seriously, thanks again to tannin. Fungi, unable to manufacture food themselves, must live off some other substance. In doing so, they cause the dead tissues to decay and often kill the living. A brown heart rot, for instance, in gaining entry through the bark or a

*People tend to crowd around the base of the giants,
wanting to touch them but compacting the soil too
dangerously for the life and health of the trees.*

burn, will in time eat into the heartwood; and while not destroying the tree, it nevertheless ruins the wood and creates a natural fuel that when ignited, will smolder internally for weeks or months.

Most trees are subject to injury and death by some kind of insect, and the redwood is not totally immune. It has to fight off a tiny pest that tends to reduce the bark just under the surface to a powder, although not endangering the tree. And while the sapwood isn't necessarily immune to termites, lumber cut from the tannin-rich heartwood will resist their attacks for countless years, even in the high humidity of the tropics where they continuously reduce wood construction and jungle growth to humus. One thing is certain: redwood lumber will be sturdy and useful long after other woods have crumbled into dust.

Although a redwood tree can survive a series of raging forest fires and resist infection and decay, it is no match for its worst enemy —man.

With travel and visitation to the giants increasing year after year, the soil around the base of the trees is becoming so trampled and compacted that the feeder roots are crushed and the flow of water and nutrients up through the trunks to the crowns is blocked. The bark of the surface roots becomes so gashed and bruised by people climbing over them to have their pictures taken, that barriers have had to be erected to restrain the hordes of sightseers. Understandably, the park services have had to limit automobile access, and new construction, and even camping under the big trees. This policy applies in many groves of both coast and Sierra, where some roads have been closed to traffic and entire beaten-up areas gradually fenced off and "put to bed" for years, to rest and recover from man's over-enthusiastic attentions. This way, winters will loosen the soil and the nutritious ground litter will remain undisturbed for a long time. Hopefully, the crowns of the giants will then stop turning brown, and begin regaining their healthy green. The forest floor, once more rich in nutrients, will become soft and springy. Small plants and flowers of all kinds will reappear, as very slowly the forest recovers from "people erosion."

The next time you return to your favorite redwood park and find your oldtime campsite closed, be patient and understanding. It is resting and rejuvenating so your grandchildren and theirs will have these same giants to enjoy, just as you and your children have.

Cloudsweepers
by the Sea

In the cool moist forests along the Pacific, where groves are dark and the humus thick, how do redwood seeds settle into the soil to start life? With so little sun penetrating to the forest floor, how do any that might have taken root grow into tall giants? Mostly they don't.

Few seeds find their way to mineral soil through the forest litter that has been accumulating for centuries. Most young redwoods rise as shoots from the root collar around the base of a burned or injured giant. Redwoods are one of the very few conifers to reproduce in this way—certainly the only one of commercial value to do so. Even the Big Tree of the Sierra cannot. With them it's seeds or else.

Not all the feathery little sprouts rising in a ring around the mother tree will survive. Competition for the vitally important sunlight and moisture is fierce and decisive, so gradually they thin out until only a dozen or so of various sizes—and the hardiest—remain. These "fairy circles" grow much faster than do seedlings, eventually becoming big redwoods, which, after reaching maturity can produce fairy circles of their own. Small wonder that this forest is known as the ever-living one.

Many stumps left after logging sprout almost immediately. Well-managed cutover areas not laid waste by overburning produce redwoods 100 to 200 feet tall and up to 6 feet in diameter in 40 to 60 years from such sprouting. In a single year they can add 2 inches to their diameter and 18 inches to their height and well within your lifetime rise as tall as a thousand-year old giant. Where moderate burning of slash is conducted after logging, uncovering the soil and sterilizing it by destroying all disease and fungi, seeds take hold readily, and together with the sprouting stumps, soon develop into a splendid new stand of young redwoods.

In an undisturbed forest, one not altered by man, the mother tree eventually falls, but by then the young ones clustered around her may have been growing for several hundred years. Even though the old giant's passing will leave a big hole in the sky and of course another in the ground, the rains of many winters will smooth the soil where she was uprooted until at last there is only a gentle depression within the family circle. You are bound to come upon many such "craters" among the coast redwoods. Some are large enough that vacationers like to set up camp and even pitch their tents in them.

If some day, in sauntering along a trail, you discover not a circle but a straight line of young trees, don't be surprised. After a big one topples, some of its limbs grow to become sizeable redwoods, and seeds of various kinds falling into its trunk may take hold. In time it may be completely covered by the litter of passing years, but the little ones will go on to take their places in the understory—a living candelabra. Often their roots straddle the trunk to reach mineral soil. Of such are the amazing regenerating powers of this forest.

Although coast redwoods are much more prolific by stump and root sprouting, they can reproduce by seed when they are about 20 years old. Between late November and February, redwoods of coast and Sierra burst into bloom. Male and female flowers appear separately on different branches of the same tree, and for a time, thick yellow clusters of both seem to change the color of the foliage. The female flowers receive the soft yellow pollen loosed from the male flowers and, after a few weeks of fertilization, begin to form into little cones that when fully developed are brown and about an inch long. At the end of the following summer they mature, opening to shed their 50 to 60 seeds to the fall winds. These can be seen drifting by the billions onto the ground below. Most travel hundreds of feet; some, several miles. Tiny, winged, it takes an average of 125,000 to make a pound.

Viable seeds in soil bared by fire, flood or animal and human activity germinate there in 20 to 30 days. The crucial thing for them is somehow to survive the first few months or year, when their tender shoots are prime favorites of cutworms, insects, squirrels, and deer. On an undisturbed forest floor, any seedling trying to struggle up through the heavily organic duff has even greater problems. It is almost sure to be destroyed by disease or fungi before it ever gets far enough to qualify as an hors d'oeuvre for neighborhood wildlife.

No doubt you have noticed almost pure stands of giants on protected alluvial flats. That is *climax forest*, where all other species of trees have been crowded out. There the redwoods seem to grow the largest and tallest, partly because of periodic winter flooding, enabling them to absorb and store many thousands of gallons of water in their trunks and thus counteract the enormous evaporation of the dry months. During such flood times, deposits of silt and loam many feet thick are laid down in the groves, smothering the roots of companion

Richardson Grove on the Eel River in Humboldt
County, one of the really magnificent riverside
flats of coastal giants.

*Winding its peaceful way through canyon and valley
to the sea, the Eel River beckons the visitor to come
bathing or fishing or photographing—or just looking.*

trees of other species, which become dropouts. How then can the giants maintain life with their root systems buried so deeply in the alluvium?

To begin with, the river sediments are apparently rich in nutritious elements. Adding to this advantage, the redwoods after each flooding develop a brand new root system that will adapt to the new and higher ground level and take over the work of the lower roots, now dying. First, vertical roots are sent up, then feeder roots extend horizontally just below the surface to scout out the nutrients of the recently arrived topsoil and humus. Sometimes you can see their tiny tips sticking up. This amazing capability is one more reason why redwoods persist where other trees are eliminated—also why giants appear in dark, pure stands along the rivers, preserved there for you to enjoy.

In places less prone to flooding, many kinds of trees grow in association with the redwoods according to their tolerance of shade, soil, and moisture conditions.

Along the open creek bottoms, the broadleaf maple, red alder, sycamore, and willow provide splashes of warm color in the autumn when almost all else is evergreen. Standing tall and splendid beside the redwoods are their most impressive and abundant companion, the stately Douglas firs. Together, they form a lofty canopy.

Then at various locations, depending upon the latitude, elevation, exposure, soil, and climate, grow members of the understory: the smaller redwoods and lesser conifers, the yew, western hemlock, grand fir, Sitka spruce, and Port Orford cedar; the broadleaf trees like the California laurel or bay or pepperwood; the twisting red-trunked madrone with its paper-thin bark peeling off each summer; several kinds of oaks, most prolific of which is the tanbark.

Down at the shrub level live the splashy and colorful azalea and rhododendron, the showy buckeye and dogwood, the toyon, salal, and California hazel. Here flourish masses of vines and bushes laden in the summer months with fruit for people and animals to harvest—the Oregon grape, huckleberry, salmonberry, thimbleberry, gooseberry, blackberry, raspberry, and Himalayaberry.

Out of the humus springs an infinite variety of ground covers —the carpet of oxalis, a myriad of wildflowers, mosses, and ferns.

Each member of this layered ecosystem is in itself a distinct personality that plays a special part in setting off the masterpiece of them all, the redwood giant with its fluted columns soaring up into the sky.

The dark, old-growth redwood forest is not as densely populated with bird and animal life as many people suppose. With so little sunshine, food is not as available as in the more open places. But once a heavily shaded area is opened, letting in light and air, and the soil is upturned by logging, construction, or a natural disaster such as a windfall, landslide, flood, or fire, vegetation springs up in profusion and animal life moves in. Until if and when this happens, most of the wild ones, both predator and prey, like it best at the forest edges. These you find along the roads, beside streams, lagoons, and meadows—places where plant life, rich in protein, abounds, attracting elk, deer —sometimes bear and mountain lion—and a whole host of smaller creatures.

Let's say a wildfire sweeps through a vast area, consuming everything except the big redwoods, saved by their thick, flame-resistant bark. The scene is one of total desolation. Eventually winds blow away the ashes and may also be strong enough to topple some of the old giants, which, because of the fire destroying all else around them, are

Jedediah Smith. The silent Coastal Redwood forests quickly make one forget the noise of the outside world.

28   Adventures in the Redwoods

A Giant Among Men

SEQUOYAH, A CHEROKEE INDIAN, although completely illiterate, created a written language for his tribe and did it alone, solely through the powers of his own mind. Because of this, his people, also illiterate, learned to read and write.

Born about 1760 to an Indian mother and a transient white father in the Cherokee village of Tuskegee, Tennessee, Sequoyah as a child was crippled and soon left fatherless. While other young braves hunted and fished and played games, Sequoyah was forced to watch. Alone much of the time, he grew introspective, brooding about the treatment of his people by the white man,

until, emerging into manhood, he decided to do something about it.

On a trip east to the American colonies, Sequoyah happened to see a silversmith at work and became so fascinated that he determined to master the craft. But how would he ever take the new knowledge home with him? Because Cherokees only spoke their language, he would have to store the details in his mind and then remember them later. This he did so well that he was not only able to set up his own shop but also to make the necessary tools.

Soon Indians coming from everywhere to watch him work forgot to pity him for being crippled. Instead, they were lost in

now isolated and consequently vulnerable. In the autumn, seeds from the few survivors plus those drifting in from a distance, fall into the newly exposed and sterilized soil.

Then come the winter rains. Erosion caused by the heavy downpour topples more big redwoods and washes away millions upon millions of seeds; yet some remain to take root. Meanwhile, any burn-damaged giants not too old to do so, have begun sprouting a new generation around their bases.

At the same time, shrubs of every kind, along with the seeds of different conifers and broadleaf trees, have begun taking hold with vigor. Of the trees, the conifer seedlings rise more slowly. For perhaps decades they submit to the shade of the broadleafed ones, but likewise benefit from their protection from the elements. Finally, though, the evergreens overtake the others, and responding to the full glow of the sun, soon tower above everything else. But here and there along the way, the spruces and hemlocks drop out of the race, leaving the homestretch to the Douglas fir and the redwood. Of this pair of finalists, you know which one stretches tallest into the sky.

With the passing of centuries, the lofty redwood crowns tend to

(continued from p. 29)

admiration for his skill in fashioning ornaments that amazed and delighted them. Sequoyah's silverwork has never been surpassed in Craftsmanship and beauty by that of any other American Indian.

Yet he was not happy because the white man kept abusing and cheating the Cherokees. He thought long and seriously about how he might change all this.

Earlier, while visiting the colonies, he had seen the white man's "talking leaves". Since these leaves seemed to say things to all who looked upon them, he resolved to create something similar for his people.

Forthwith, at the age of 49, Sequoyah put away his silvercraft tools and set his mind to originating a kind of alphabet for the Cherokees. But because he was often seen making strange carvings on the bark of trees, the Indians began to think evil spirits had taken possession of the man. Scorned and friendless, Sequoyah nevertheless struggled on, at first making a symbol for *every word* of the Cherokee language until his symbols mounted into the thousands. Disgusted, Sequoyah threw his hard work away and started all over again, this time separating Cherokee speech into *individual sounds* with a written symbol for each. At the end of twelve years he had broken the

interlock, forming the canopy that permits little sun to penetrate as far as the forest floor. The old giants, past their prime, can no longer produce seeds that germinate and in their dense shade, other trees, many shrubs, and much of the ground cover gradually dies out, leaving the big over-mature redwoods in almost pure stands. This process from seed or sprout to climax forest is known as plant succession.

When you realize that these trees you gaze up at in awe cannot be those of dinosaur times but thousands of generations later, doesn't it make you wonder what comes next for the groves of splendid giants on the riverside flats—mighty, to be sure, but unable any longer to perpetuate their kind? Where will plant succession go from here now that the latest element, man, has arrived to trample the life-giving upper six inches of soil and destroy the humus; to mold the landscape to his own assorted needs by cutting, clearing, and preserving large areas? How will this magnificent ecosystem remain in balance when there are no longer any young redwoods springing up in the groves to carry on the forest grandeur after the old ones go, as they inevitably will?

The coast redwood was the first to achieve scientific identity when in 1974 Archibald Menzies, a Scottish botanist with the Vancouver Expedition collected foliage, seeds, and cones near Santa Cruz

Cherokee language down into only 85 such symbols. Some he had copied from an American newspaper found alongside a trail; the others he designed.

Still fearing evil spirits, none of the Cherokees would have anything to do with Sequoyah's alphabet—none, that is, except two young braves who agreed to be taught; and they really didn't intend—or expect—to learn, for both had set out to verify what everyone else thought—that Sequoyah was mad.

Much to their surprise, they found that the writing actually was going to work; that they could learn to speak with one another on the talking leaves as did the white man. On winged feet the young braves sped back to their village to spread the news.

Life for the Cherokees changed quickly now as the excited Indians put everything aside and in a few months learned to read. Eventually they published their own newspaper and translated parts of the Bible, and when the Great White Father in Washington D.C. called for a Cherokee representative to come to his council fire, Sequoyah was chosen. In the nation's capital he was received with honor and respect.

The English language took 3000 years to become what it is. The Cherokee's written language was the work of one man over just

and took them back to London's Natural History Museum for study. Yet the new tree was not officially named until 1824 when an English botanist, A. B. Lambert, decided it was an evergreen in the same genus (*Taxodiaceae*) as the deciduous, cone-bearing bald cypress of our Southeast and Mexico. So he classified it the *Taxodium sempervirens*—or evergreen taxodium.

Some years later, in 1847, Stephen Endlicher, an Austrian botanist, decided the tree was not a taxodium at all but an entirely new genus, although certainly a sempervirens ever-green. Forthwith, he initiated the new genus by honoring Sequoyah, a Cherokee Indian. Latinizing the name, Endlicher called the redwood the *Sequoia sempervirens*.

Afterwards, upon the discovery of a mammoth tree in the Sierra, and figuring that this was still another genus, English botanist John Lindley settled upon *Wellingtonia gigantea* for the big red giant, this to honor the Duke of Wellington, who had defeated Napoleon at Waterloo. But American botanists, not to be outdone, honored their national hero by choosing the name *Sequoia washingtonia*.

Then along came French botanist Descaine to get into the act with *Sequoia gigantea* for the Sierra redwood, and so that one has

(continued from p. 31)
the span of twelve years.

When Sequoyah reached seventy years of age, he decided to journey into the western wilderness, wishing to teach the Indians there; in fact, to unite ALL Indians in a common language.

One day he set out on foot from Oklahoma, with him a young brave. Together they plodded through wind and blistering heat until winter came. Blizzards swept across the southern plains. In the mountains the snows deepened. Wolves circled and howled. Somewhere along the way the young brave weakened and died, leaving Sequoyah to push on alone.

High in the Mexican Sierra he came to the end of his trail. Not knowing that this was his last campfire, he huddled and watched the smoke curl upwards. Slowly the flame of his magnificent spirit flickered, then, like his campfire, died. In time the wind and earth covered his remains but left nothing to mark his final resting place.

Still, what finer monument to his memory could there be than a living one—our giant redwoods named in his honor. An honor magnificently deserved.

---

remained until 1939 when more careful studies by the late Professor John T. Buckholtz indicated that it should be classified in a separate genera. The giganteas were then renamed *sequoiadendron giganteum*. And as of now, that's how the matter stands.

Conquest of the Redwoods

California's northcoast Indians tell that the redwoods were there long before the very first of their people came. And they will also add that their forebears generally avoided the inner forest because it was dark and foreboding, and anyway, the food they sought was best found around the fringes, the streams, and the sea. Then, too, some believed that the giants contained the spirits of their ancestors, so they tended to hang back rather than go in and make themselves at home. They did, however, appreciate the easy workability of redwood and used it for making such things as bowls and platters, stools, and boxes for their personal effects. Roots they wove into baskets; bark slabs they fashioned into shelters or shredded it into skirts for their women. When they died, their graves were covered with redwood, and a big booming fire of redwood lighted their way into the next world.

How did they fell such trees? They never needed to. Trees of all sizes lay on the forest floor, and after winter storms, on the beaches where river and tide had dumped them. All the Indians had to do to sever a desired log length was to set fires that would burn through the bole. Once the log was free they went to work with stone hammers and wedges of sharpened elk antlers to split out slabs for building their sweathouses. To make a dugout canoe, they hollowed a log with fire. Then they chopped away at it with a cutting tool of a mussel shell blade until it had been satisfactorily shaped to withstand years of fishing along the coast and paddling upriver for trade with the inland brothers.

The year 1769 probably marks the first sighting of redwoods by men other than Indians, at least those arriving by land. These were the Spanish of the Portola Expedition riding north from San Diego. That October, as they approached the Pajaro River near present day Watsonville, Fray Juan Crespi, the diarist, wrote that they were traversing "low hills and plains forested with very high trees of red color not known to us."—and added: "In this region there is a great abundance of these trees and because none of the expedition recognizes them, they are named from their color" (*Palo colorado*).

An old photograph, taken in the 1890's, shows two loggers about to fell a huge redwood.

In establishing their chain of missions, presidios, and pueblos, and laying claim to Alta California, the Spanish and the Mexicans who followed were near redwoods but not actually *of* them. With simple ax and whipsaw they cut whichever trees were handy for the making of furniture, utensils, doors, and window frames. Their principal building material, adobe, was more discouraging to hostile Indians, who practiced a little light arson. Eventually, though, they did discover the fire-resistant qualities of redwood and its great strength and durability and thereafter hewed out huge beams of it with which to support their heavy tile roofs. And because redwood was found to be remarkably free of knots, straight-grained, water-resistant, neither warping nor splintering, they began to hew it into planks for aqueducts, and vats for hide tanning and the storage of water and wine.

The Russians, who arrived in California about 1811 to clean the coast of sea otter, used wood extensively. They built Fort Ross overlooking the sea north of the Russian River mouth, and it was a redwood fort—stockade, chapel, commanders headquarters, homes, every-

*An ox team dragging redwood logs over a greased
"skid road" in 1881.*

This early logging train is pulling two redwoods,
sawed into logs to fit flatcars.

thing. Back of the fort they felled trees up to 20 feet in diameter, and right there today is some of the oldest second-growth in redwood country. A boring in one big tree showed 135 rings and others may be even older. In fact some have grown big and old enough to be cut the second time, making it third-growth! The Russians even tried ship-building down in their tiny cove, but learned the hard way that red-wood in saltwater expands more than an inch lengthwise and contracts less than an inch sidewise, and therefore did nothing for flotation at sea.

It took the Yankees from the east coast with their can-do talents and energy to set redwood logging in motion, beginning in Monterey County about 1834 and working steadily northward. At first this was done with two-man whipsaws and much sweating over one plank at a time, sawed from a log laid across an open pit. And at 25¢ an hour!

Later, in the 1840's, ships brought machinery and tools around the Horn, enabling lumbermen to build watermills and later steam-powered mills in the Santa Cruz area, on both sides of San Francisco

Hee-li

DID YOU KNOW THAT BECAUSE of a bug-size foulup neither Columbus nor Leif Ericsson but a Chinese may have discovered America? And the redwoods, too? Should you feel an urge to close your mind, consider this:

Supposedly in 217 B.C. a Chinese navigator named Hee-li, in plying his coastal trade—off China, that is—was tossed far off his course in a terrific storm. Having survived, and anxious to get home, he headed westward, so he thought. But somehow a cockroach had wandered into his compass, got wedged under the needle, and stuck the darn thing. Despite the protests of his men, Hee-li stubbornly did as the compass directed, even though the sun appeared to be setting on the wrong horizon.

Almost 100 days of nothing but water followed, and then— LAND! Still, it was not the homeland of China that Hee-li and his men set foot on, but a strange country of dark towering forests around a vast inlet, which they explored.

Twenty-one centuries after that historic bumbling, an American missionary to China found a musty manuscript stashed away in the archives at Shensi. In it was the description of the unplanned voyage across the Pacific to shores populated with red men, and of Hee-li's exploration of the red-trunked giant trees and the inlet that reached far into a continent unfamiliar to his Chinese countrymen.

Bay, and along the Russian River. Even so, this was slow business, and the total cutting at that time made no noticeable inroads into the total mass of redwood forest estimated to have been around 2 million acres all together.

Only a couple of hundred residents lived in San Francisco in the 1840's and the few other settlements were small and far apart. Nearby, dense forests stood formidable and for the most part unexplored and undisturbed until suddenly the cry GOLD! went up across the country. Then things did change. Men swarmed in by land and sea, left the bay clogged with abandoned ships, and headed for the Mother Lode. In support of the miners, came men of other skills and objectives to clear away forests for farming and livestock raising and the construction of houses and business buildings. In all the uproar, the hills surrounding San Francisco Bay were denuded of what had been some of the grandest of redwood forests. According to pre turn-of-the-century writings by distinguished scientists who examined the stumps, the hills and canyons behind present-day Oakland must have been populated with

*Fort Ross on Sonoma County's redwood coast, was
founded by Russian fur traders, 1812-41. The
restored Russian Orthodox chapel is now a favorite stopover for thousands of visitors.*

the most magnificent forest of all. In a single area, most of the trees had
been at least 16 feet in diameter, a great number exceeding 20 feet well
above breast height. One stump, that of a triple tree, measured 57 feet
across—probably in its time the mightiest living thing on the face of
the earth. In less than a decade not much of them remained; in less
time than that, more than 100,000 people had passed into and through
San Francisco, perhaps half of that number settling in the immediate
area. So early in the 1850's "cut and get out" logging flourished to meet
the mushrooming need.

　　Farther north, up at Humboldt Bay and Crescent City, more
enterprising men moved in to harvest some of the seemingly endless
supply of redwood. Most of the mills were situated at the mouths of the
rivers. In that way the cuts from the big riverside trees could be rolled
into the water at the logging site upstream, left there until high water
rafted them down to be sawed into lumber. From there it would be

loaded by chute and cable from the cliffs onto two-masted windjammers—later steam schooners—plying the coast south to San Francisco. As weather permitted, these rugged little vessels put into every cove or "dog hole" (where there was just room enough for a dog to turn around) and took on the mill's stack of redwood posts, shakes, railroad ties, and siding.

All of this was slow backbreaking labor, especially the mammoth job of felling the big redwoods. To begin with, old-time lumberjacks from the eastern and southern forests found themselves stymied by giant trees many times larger than any they had ever dreamed of. Not for long though.

American ingenuity being what it was, the men cut notches in the trunks a dozen or more feet above the root flare, where the diameter wasn't quite as monstrous, and inserted springboards on which to stand while tackling their problem. If in balancing there, two choppers with heavy, double-bitted axes whacked away 12 hours a day for a week, they could bring the giant down. But the ax handle had to be long enough for the head to reach the center of a tree—six or seven feet at least. Quite a challenge, this, even to experienced Paul Bunyan woodsmen. For the first century of redwood logging, a razor-sharp ax was their pride and joy and lifeblood. It was honed as carefully as if it were a surgeon's knife.

In those days no bedding was laid for the felling of a big tree. Down it went with a thundering crash, taking dozens of other trees along. And after the huge bole was cleaned of limbs, and bucked or blasted into 40 to 50-ton lengths of only the best wood, the rest was abandoned where it lay and the loggers moved on, leaving the scene with all the parklike beauty of a battlefield.

At that time, redwood acreage was cheap. Selling for between $1 and $5 an acre, it provided an attractive come-on not only to lumbermen but also to pioneering farmers and ranchers who had the wild idea they could clear the land and be under way in no time. It took years for them to realize that redwood was different from other trees and to recognize the stubborn resistance of redwood itself, whose stumps kept sprouting and resprouting in defiance of the ax, the torch, even dynamite. Even so, the redwood met its match in the persistence of the Yankees, and some acreage was finally cleared enough to give way to crops and pasture.

Yankee ingenuity and energy also brought in oxen to drag big logs over greased skid roads of half-buried, widely-spaced logs laid crosswise. However, this rugged breed of men still had to face really overwhelming redwood country odds like raging fires that time and time again destroyed their mills, and winter floods that wiped out logging roads, mills, and millponds filled with perhaps a year's cut. Compounding it all were the windy storm fronts off the Pacific. In moments they could make matchwood of steam-driven schooners, loaded to the gunwales with lumber, before they could clear the cliffs at the rivermouth. And granting that a ship made it safely and expensively to San Francisco, then around the Horn to the eastern seaboard, murderous competition from the lumbermen there lurked, waiting. In the 20 years between 1863 and 1883, nearly two billion board feet of redwood passed through the Port of San Francisco, and millions of feet more were shipped directly from the redwood coast to Australia and the Orient.

High stakes, these, but in the tall timber there were men to match. The big quake of 1906 that flattened many a mill and San Francisco to boot, only reinforced the lumberman's true grit and the city's sense of urgency to rebuild. By then, technological progress was marching on in grand style.

With the advent of the 1880's, long crosscut handsaws had begun to replace axes and the skidroad oxen were giving way to steam-powered donkey engines that winched logs by cable from the steep slopes to flatcars, there to be yarded to the mills by small steam locomotives. Later came the ultimate—the bull donkey's high lead cables that swung logs through the air to the loading platforms near the donkey.

And that wasn't all. The mills, too, boasted their slice of progress when double circular saws, working simultaneously from above and below, sliced through logs six feet in diameter and were later succeeded by whining bandsaws that could carve up logs of any size. Old-growth logging now boomed. The earth shook as the big ones containing a fantastic number of houses crashed earthward. With the stepped-up production, more and more lumbermen began to develop dollar signs for eyes.

Meanwhile, back in the forest, there had to be some burning of slash—the bark and foliage and splintered debris—in order to extricate the prime logs. These fires, if they didn't break loose and run wild, usually succeeded in consuming all the young seedlings and saplings just starting to grow, setting back the forest's natural regeneration, sometimes for decades. But who cared! Didn't redwood forests stretch as far as eye could reach? Why then be picky about a few thousand big trees!

After the building of the Transcontinental Railroad and the Panama Canal, more redwood than ever departed from California.

A mule train carrying a redwood log prior to the turn of the century.

Up until World War II destructive steam logging was still snorting across tens of thousands of acres. Long before then, however, concern for the future had surfaced. Forestry had become a science and foresters were beginning to censor haphazard logging and burning. Even the loggers had started to speak of such things as sustained yield and regeneration, whether from pangs of conscience or from the sensible economics of how to stay in business by seeing to it that their vast tracts of land would be continuously productive.

Studies were made that recommended less destructive logging, better protection of cuts from fire, flood, and grazing, and greater consideration for trees trying to seed and sprout. More than this, by the turn of the century and in the name of generations yet unborn, groups of alarmed citizens were protesting against the wanton butchery, the waste, the fouling of streams—the rape of entire watersheds and the utter disregard for even minimum reforestation.

Two decades passed. All the while the protests of newly-formed conservation groups were growing louder and stronger—loud and strong enough to have raised the kind of clout that brought about the preservation of big redwood acreages "in a state of nature" for all time to come.

*Early loggers stripped the forests as seen in this
1919 photograph.*

A number of lumber companies joined in a reforestation program. By the mid-1930's redwood nurseries had sprung up at several points in redwood country and millions upon millions of seedlings had been planted. Selective logging began, by federal regulation leaving five seed trees to the acre. Mature and over-mature giants were cut, opening the canopy so the younger and smaller "leave trees" at last enjoying sunlight, could take off skyward, to be harvested later.

Chainsaws now lightened the work of loggers, heavy Caterpillar tractors and big lumber trucks capable of transporting the largest logs, slowly replaced steam logging equipment. But not until the early 1950's did the majority of big lumber companies start selective logging and honest-to-goodness scientific forest management.

At the end of World War II California underwent massive changes when the population increased and shifted. Building construction boomed as never before—and with it the demand for lumber. Some companies, with total disregard for the future, quickly laid waste to thousands of acres of forest. Others, directed by thinking men who were desirous of perpetuating a renewable natural resource in addition to succeeding in business, moved forward by hiring professional forest scientists, systematically and highly trained at the University of California School of Forestry. They became motivated to manage their holdings as a crop instead of mining and then abandoning them. Some even joined in saving redwoods by setting aside their groves of old growth; waiting years, all the while paying heavy taxes until the groves could be purchased and dedicated as parks for the wonder and enjoyment of the American people.

The Forest Practices Act, passed by the California State Legislature in 1945, establishing a framework for voluntary compliance with good forest practices of cutting, reforestation, and protection, was later declared unconstitutional. The new act of 1973, one of the toughest in the United States, authorized the appointment of a nine-member State Board of Forestry—three from the industry, one from the livestock ranks, and five from the general public who have no financial interests in timberlands. Each of the several districts formed has its own technical advisory board selected from the public; each must submit a harvesting plan to the State Forester; each has to abide by regulations assuring the continuous growth of commercial forests and prescribing proper attention to the protection of soil, air, wildlife, fish and water resources.

Five years after the passage of the first Forest Practices Act—1950—the year of California's statehood centennial, redwood tree farms came into being. During the 1960's especially, great progress was made in that direction until now there are more than 120 such farms, their owners pledged to perpetual growth. Today, with most of the major companies, conservation concerns are operating hand-in-hand with those involving sales and profits.

Logging and milling nowadays allows for little waste. Even the mountains of bark peeled off by jetstream in the millpond has a hundred uses. It is ground or shredded into insulation against heat, cold, and sound for home, industry, and refrigeration; for packing material, and because it conditions soil—for garden compost and orchid potting. Among the other uses are roofing, oil well drilling, in detergents, bed blankets, and filters of sewage disposal plants, just to name a few.

After the chainsaws have finished in the woods, any remaining debris is ground up into chips for gardens and patios, into hardboard for construction purposes, but most important of all into pulp for paper products. Even the sawdust is compressed into logs for campfires and barbecues.

Because redwood neither shrinks nor swells very much, it is unexcelled for outdoor construction where extremes of weather can be expected. And because heartwood stands strong and resists decay and insects such as termites, builders find it particularly valuable for structural underpinning. Moreover, it is lightweight and free of pitch and resin and as fire-resistant as a softwood can be. This was discovered in the fire following the 1906 San Francisco earthquake, when most of the unscathed buildings were those of redwood. Durability is the word for such lumber. Used for one purpose for many years, it can then be recycled and turned into something entirely different.

Fences, grapestakes, tanks, and silos of redwood outlast by many years those made of other woods. You find redwood in dams, in irrigation flumes and water pipes, shingles, bridges, trestles, waste disposal systems; wharves and their pilings, patios and their furniture, stadiums and their seats—and countless other places of outdoor construction.

A telephone pole installed near Healdsburg in 1884 was recently removed, not that it had deteriorated, but simply because a taller one was required to carry more lines. You might say the old redwood pole was merely retired. In Los Angeles in 1968 and much to everyone's surprise, a mile of 12 to 18-inch tongue-in-groove redwood stave water conduit of the kind installed in the 1880's was unearthed. Almost 15,000 feet of the conduit was still in service at the time, as well preserved as the day it was laid. It, too, was retired. Due to heavy urbanization, water officials felt that iron or steel would better carry

The modern mills use every part of the logs.

The Church Built from One Tree

IN SANTA ROSA STANDS A UNIQUE church with a 70 foot spire, constructed from the wood of a single redwood tree, and made famous by Believe-It-Or-Not Robert L. Ripley in his memorable cartoons of world oddities. Felled near Guerneville in 1875, the giant measured 18 feet in diameter and had lived perhaps 2000 years or more.

During the nearly ten decades the little Gothic structure served as Santa Rosa's First Baptist Church, it accommodated 300 people at a time. But eventually, as the city grew, a larger edifice became a necessity.

In 1970, the then abandoned Church of One Tree was converted into not only an Historical Landmark, but also a home for the Ripley Memorial Museum—a fitting dedication. You see, Ripley had been born in Santa Rosa in 1893, and its citizens, wished to honor him—not just as a collector of world oddities, but more personally, as a man, one of their more illustrious townfolk.

That's why this church means just a bit more than do the five permanent Believe-It-Or-Not Museums in New York, Chicago, San Francisco, St. Augustine, Fla., and Niagra Falls, Canada.

---

the enormous pressures now required.

Once seasoned, redwood is impervious to acid and alkalis solutions and so is excellent in the manufacture of soaps, ink, and whiskey. And edibles such as olives, pickles, cheeses, wines, and fruit juices may be safely stored in redwood casks and tanks without absorbing the flavor or odor of the wood.

Since this wonder wood is so workable as to texture and its color so rich, it can readily be sawed, chipped, or carved, then smoothed into a satin-like patina. No paint, stain, or varnish is necessary for finishing, although it takes paint and stains well. Nails stay in, glue applies easily, and woodworking tools shape it with the minimum of effort. All kinds of unique gifts, both useful and ornamental, can be fashioned from the remarkably straight-grained wood as well as from the burls—those knotty birds-eye growths that bulge from root and trunk and make beautiful and valuable lamps, bowls, bookends, and tabletops.

Not all of the growths are true burls, however, for some are actually a form of scar tissue or "overgrowth" resulting from an injury. A real burl is a hard conglomarate of many dormant buds. The original single bud sprang from the tree's pith but failed to develop into a branch. As the tree aged, it divided and redivided until a lump was

Santa Rosa's famed Church Built from One Tree
stands beside the city's Julliard Park. Now a museum,
it is open to the public 11 a.m. to 4 p.m. daily.

Conquest of the Redwoods

Roadside Plantings

AND DON'T BE SURPRISED IF IN your travels through the smoggy parts of California you see extensive roadside plantings of redwood. Some, apparently unaffected by smog alerts and a stream of passing exhausts are busy bearing out the fact that they are the fastest growing conifer in America. Long ago, landscape architects of the State Division of Highways began searching for smog-tolerant trees with which to border their ugly freeways. Survivors of their experiments to date are the sugar pines and redwoods, both coast and Sierra.

While smog often kills pines and firs outright, it usually weakens them so that they easily fall victim to insects and disease.

Redwoods do not die from such attacks.

So you will doubtless notice young ones rising 2 to 8 feet a year beside our wide ribbons of concrete in places from San Bernardino to Sacramento and the Santa Clara Valley. That's right—even in the dry climes of the southland, where they are tenderly and frequently hand-watered to make up for some of the natural watering of their own natural habitat.

Yet you can find plantings of them there, too. Beside Highway 101 between Petaluma and Healdsburg, where once there grew no trees, redwoods are thriving almost within reach of whizzing steel.

---

formed that may be seen on trunk, limb, or around the base.

Burls come in all sizes, those on the base sometimes weighing tons. These are prized by woodworkers, who cut and shape them into handsome birds-eye tabletops, trays, lamps, salad bowls, and book ends. Small burls, having no commercial value, are sold simply for their sprouting. Place one of them in a shallow dish of water, and depending upon the number of buds within it, feathery fern-like greens will rise to delight you. Care for it well, and it could provide several years of redwood forest beauty in your home.

Once in a while a burl develops into a root that, when planted, grows into a tree; but these are rare. Remember to be amazed if yours does.

There is much left to learn and do in improving sustained yield on commercial lands, managing in such a way as to fill the skyrocketing insistance on forest products and at the same time guaranteeing natural wild beauty and perpetuation of redwood forests. What a stupendous challenge not only to lumberman, forest scientist, conservationist, federal and state forest and park services alike, but also to the public, who

Some burls are so huge they may weigh 40 or 50 tons.

Giant Redwood towering two hundred feet above
the forest floor and the attendant National Park
Range at Muir Woods National Monument (Marin
County) just forty-five minutes north of San Francisco.

must somehow equate their material demands with their aesthetic desires—and live with both. And let us remember, too, about the oxygen the trees release for us to breathe, the watershed they hold down, and the peace and quiet and sanctuary they offer to human and animal life.

Preserving the Scene
for Man's Enjoyment

In the early days along the coast and in the decades following the Gold Rush, when the sequoias were first discovered, few men thought about saving redwoods just because they were inspiring to see and enjoy and should be preserved as a natural heritage for coming generations. The giants, quite simply, were there to be taken for granted—and taken for lumber.

The first protest came from the Sierra, where between the Civil War and the turn of the century it seemed every last giant would be cut in man's greedy stampede toward wealth. No matter that the Big Tree, far too brittle for most uses, shattered to pieces when it fell or that even the pieces were too monstrous to handle. To a pop-eyed woodsman a small acreage of such monsters surely contained whole towns, and therefore more gold than the placers.

When the Civil War ended, releasing thought to turn in other directions, "Save the sequoias!" was heard loud and clear all the way to Washington D.C. Despite the outcry, the sequoias, out of sight in the far, far West, were out of mind as well. The ring of ax on wood continued to echo ominously through the groves of the Sierra.

But President Lincoln had heard and he had listened and then responded by transferring the Mariposa Grove of Big Trees in Yosemite from Public Domain to the state foresters to be protected for all time—the nation's first state park.

In 1890 Yosemite, Sequoia, and General Grant Grove (now a part of Kings Canyon National Park) were set aside as our first national parks after Yellowstone. Vociferous private citizens and well-organized conservation groups, coordinating with government, acquired thousands of acres of the finest groves and deeded them to public ownership and protection. In time, 92 percent of the Big Trees were brought under federal, state, or local jurisdiction, either as forests or parks and logging in the sequoias became a thing of the past.

The movement to save some of the tall coastal forests from ax and saw got under way much later, beginning in earnest in the twentieth century with the work of three men in the Santa Cruz Mountains south of San Francisco. The first two, J. W. Welch and Henry Cowell, had years before bought and permanently set aside large tracts in the San Lorenzo Canyon at Felton that contained prime stands of old-growth. And because these groves stood out dramatically from the logging butchery up and down the canyon, Welch and Cowell capitalized on the preserved beauty by turning their holdings into resorts and charging admission.

Among the visitors who came to take a look was the third man, a skilled photographer from San Jose, Andrew P. Hill, who tried to take pictures but was prevented from doing so by the owners, who declared this to be their prerogative. Angrily, Hill protested. These trees, he averred, should be for all the people, owned by all the people as a part of their natural heritage—and therefore free to them to enjoy. Returning to the Bay Area, Mr. Hill gathered together a group of his friends to frame some kind of protest.

Hearing of an even larger grove of redwoods a few miles upcanyon from Felton—Big Basin—about to fall to the ax, Hill and his small group of men and women entrained at once for Boulder Creek, hub of the lumbering operation. They climbed by horse-drawn carryall over a steep mountain road and down to Slippery Rock on Sempervirens Creek in the Basin and set up camp. During the days that followed, they tramped among the majestic giants, and they planned. Then at their campfire the night of May 18, 1900, they organized into the Sempervirens Club and pledged a fight to save the magnificent trees around them from destruction.

Enthusiasm knew no bounds. Publicity in newspapers and magazines sharpened the fight to save this matchless area. Armed with his photographs and a fiery determination, Hill went to Sacramento to tackle an indifferent legislature. Undaunted, he enlisted the support of Father Robert Kenna, President of Santa Clara University, an eloquent speaker. Together they pushed ahead, making stirring pleas, overcoming political obstacles that would have floored ordinary men, and securing large sums of money from public-spirited individuals, many of whom were women of great influence and means.

Amazed and impressed by the strength of the movement, a balky state legislature in 1902 finally appropriated $250,000 to purchase 3800 acres in the heart of Big Basin to be designated California Redwood Park. Thus was born California's first real state park, dedicated according to Sempervirens Club ideals to the preservation of the trees for posterity and the formation of a great park. In more detail: "to prepare a place whither our children and workmen, factory girls and others breathing all the week impure air, might, amidst the great trees and along rippling brooks, breathe pure air and rest amidst great forests, where their minds and hearts are lifted to higher, purer, nobler things."

The Sempervirens spirit and accomplishment turned out to be a sign for the times. Henry Middleton, a lumberman just outside the park, gave a 1300-acre addition to Big Basin. And up on the Russian River above San Francisco, Colonel James B. Armstrong had already decided he couldn't possibly cut such a fine grove of giants as his 440 acres. It must be kept intact, undisturbed. And so it has remained, eventually becoming a county park and in 1934 a state reserve.

In 1908 Congressman William Kent, upon learning that a little valley at the base of Mt. Tamalpais was going to be flooded by a water company, bought several hundred acres containing a prime grove of giants. First he offered it as a gift to the federal government, and was refused. Then he strove to have Congress declare it a national park, and was again refused. On a third try, President Theodore Roosevelt, using his presidential powers, saved the day by designating the gift a national monument. At Mr. Kent's request, it was named Muir Woods, honoring the famous naturalist and conservationist John Muir. This one national monument remained the only federal coast redwood park until 1968, when, after much agony and struggle, the Redwood National Park in Humboldt and Del Norte counties became a reality.

The idea of saving redwoods must have been catching, for the same year as Muir Woods, 1908, the schoolchildren of Eureka signed a petition to save some of their northern redwoods as a national park and sent it to Congress. Many of the youngsters, now men and women in their sixties, have lived to enjoy the Redwood National Park they had wanted so much so long ago.

In 1909 Calaveras Grove at the northern tip of the Sierra redwood range, came up for federal consideration. First of their kind to have been discovered, and because the Calaveras giants were massive and spectacular, much had been said and written about them. Even so, Congress, still in lockstep with its long string of rejections, left Calaveras in private hands until 1931, when resolute conservationists and the state acted together to create Calaveras Big Trees State Park.

Now the scene shifts back to the Coast Range and ahead to the year 1917. Except for steel rails between San Francisco and Eureka, and a crude road that wound through the most scenic redwood groves of Sonoma, Mendocino, Humboldt, and Del Norte counties, communication between the outside world and the northern redwood country was meager and spotty. Gradually, though, with improvements in automotive transportation, more and more people found their way to the tallest and mightiest of the coastal realm.

Among them were three distinguished men on vacation. Two were from New York—Fairfield Osborn, President of the American Museum of Natural History, and Madison Grant, Chairman of the New York Zoological Society; the third, John C. Merriam, was a paleontology professor from the University of California, later President of the Carnegie Institute of Washington D.C. What they saw when they rode along and walked through the forest excited them as it did everyone else who beheld the redwood forests' pristine majesty and grandeur. Only with these men there was a difference. They not only reveled in the beauty but also were shocked and stunned by the wanton destruction they saw everywhere—and heading directly for the lumberman's dream, the old-growth giants.

Immediately, the three went into action. They recruited other men of note and substance, including the chiefs of the national forest and park services, and organized the non-profit Save-the-Redwoods League. Franklin K. Lane, formerly Secretary of the Interior, was chosen president and the long-enduring and dedicated Newton B. Drury, Executive Secretary, a post he still holds today with continuing distinction.

The Board of Directors initiated nationwide publicity by calling for members and donations. The appeal spread quickly, and the response was enthusiastic. In the first two years, 4000 individuals of all ages and from all walks of life contributed almost $150,000. As time went along, more and more of them asked that their money go toward the purchase of a redwood national park.

The new league set up a sensible but ambitious list of objectives which included: 1. to actively assist in the establishment of a redwood national park; 2. to acquire for the preservation of scenic values the stands of redwoods along the highways then under construction; and, 3. to obtain through gift and purchase, groves of redwood threatened by lumbering operations.

The greatly respected National Geographic Society published an article setting forth those precepts and recommending definite areas for preservation, among them several groves in Mendocino and Humboldt counties, and extensive areas along Redwood Creek east of Orick, in the Lower Klamath and Smith River Basins, and in the Bull Creek-Dyerville section. About 25,000 acres of protective watershed were included.

Once again, in 1920, Congress was approached. This time the House authorized a study for a national park. The final report substantiated many of the National Geographic's recommendations, but while the bill passed the House, it died in the Senate. And that was that for the next quarter of a century.

Dismayed, but far from defeated, the League then took their crusade directly to the people, to anyone who would listen. They approached individuals with community and political influence, service clubs and other groups, state offices, and even the lumbermen, some of whom gradually became compadres in the growing movement.

For the next few years, acquisition moved right along, a piece here and a piece there, steadily adding up until the state was convinced that it should set up a matching fund framework for the establishment of parks. Its first appropriation was $300,000.

The response to this action was phenomenal. Besides all the public donations, large and small, from pennies to millions of dollars, a number of timber companies gave both lands and money and held still other prime groves in trust for future purchase when there would be money for it. The counties and several cities acted, too, contributing their efforts and some of their properties to the drive for preservation of redwoods.

At that time some of the initial groundwork was laid for state redwood parks from Sonoma to Del Norte, which included lands now in Armstrong Redwoods, Richardson Grove, Standish-Hickey Grove, Rockefeller Forest, Humboldt Redwoods, Prairie Creek, and Jedediah Smith state parks.

Today, purchases and gifts are still coming in as the League passes its half-century mark of steadily continuing funding. A plethora of memorial groves and parks bear eloquent testimony to the interest and generosity of countless individuals and organizations the country over.

Early response soon became great enough to necessitate a management body, so in 1927 a State Park Commission and a Division of Parks (now the Department of Parks and Recreation) were established and Big Basin was transferred from the State Division of Forestry to become the nucleus of the infant state park system. A $6-million bond issue, based on the principle of matching funds, and handily voted in by the electorate, added more purchase and operating muscle for the decade to come.

At the same time, the noted landscape architect, Frederick Law Olmsted, was engaged to make a lands survey. His recommendations for redwood park sites have nearly all been activated as the state and the League moved along together to acquire redwood lands, preserving the most desirable and greatly endangered ones first.

The beautiful Humboldt Redwoods State Park alongside the Redwood Highway between Garber-ville and Pepperwood containing many of the state's 400 memorial groves.

In 1938 certain royalties from state-owned oil lands accrued to park acquisition efforts and in 1945 the state simply appropriated $13-million. Several windfalls via the ballot box sweetened the fund later, among which was a $150-million bond issue in 1964—$85-million of it for land purchase.

During the 30's another type of redwood lands were extracted from private ownership. These were units under the jurisdiction of the U.S. Forest Service that totaled about 15,000 acres—not nearly the more than three quarters of a million acres originally sought. The state did better with its 47,000-acre Jackson State Forest in Mendocino County east of Fort Bragg, which is managed scientifically, and several other small areas of second-growth used largely for youth camps.

With the passing of the years, acquisition of redwood lands gained momentum, and other conservation groups organized to help save redwoods, among them the Sierra Club. Thanks to the Nature Conservancy, the public now benefits from Georgia Pacific Lumber Company's gift of a $6-million choice grove and the Marks family's 9000-acre Forest of Nisene Marks back of Aptos; thanks to the persistence of the Conservation Associates, the state now has Castle Rock State Park and an expanded Big Basin with a trail connecting the two. And there have been other and different arrangements whereby private redwood holdings have come into public ownership—a long story of tireless effort by individuals and groups—the great American way of getting things done.

Counties and cities have done their bit, too, working for the larger projects while maintaining small parks of their own. And the nine lumber companies of the California Redwood Association have opened up 350,000 acres of commercial forests under the Redwood Industry Recreation Areas program for day use—hunting, fishing, and hiking.

In 1966 federal monies of the Land and Water Conservation Fund sifted down to the coastal forests when $2-million was alloted for an extension of the Avenue of the Giants in Humboldt County. And finally, in October 1968, the long-anticipated Redwood National Park became a fact when President Johnson signed the bill, bringing to a climax a long and many-faceted controversy. Pieced together, the new park's various sections of coastline and forest, including the narrow corridor protecting the World's Tallest Trees on Redwood Creek, stretches along 55 miles of California's northwest corner. Within it are three of the state's finest redwood state parks—Prairie Creek, Del Norte Coast, and Jedediah Smith, still state-owned and operated and unquestionably the heart of the national park. Some of the other acreages, formerly in private ownership, provide the main watershed protection for this majestic old-growth.

So, as they say, this is where we came in. A redwood national park concept had been kicking around ever since 1852 and later in 1879, when a park of a million acres was recommended to the Secretary of the Interior. Purposeful and definite action materialized only after comprehensive study of resources and need by the National Park Service, funded by a Geographic Society grant.

Whether the present composite park was a conjunction of all the right segments of all the right sizes in all the right places or whether it should have included the three state parks, already safe from logging, and even though neither the industry nor the municipalities nearby nor the park services are completely happy and satisfied with the final master plan—the national park does exist today. At long last, a century of struggle to achieve the park has paid off with a 58,000-acre start.

All together, as of now, out of the two million or so acres of redwood estimated to have greeted the first comers to California, more than 180,000 acres have been set aside through the unceasing efforts and coordination of private citizens, organizations, and agencies, some by various exchanges of timber holdings.

The Save-the-Redwoods League still leads in quietly raising funds, negotiating and cooperatively bargaining with lumber interests, adding acreage after acreage to the State Park System as money becomes available. Let there be no doubt in anyone's mind that the League has fathered the California state parks. With a membership now exceeding 60,000 the League has in its fifty-plus years raised over $14-million in contributions, matched by the state, dollar for dollar, some of it appearing as memorial groves, of which there are now 400.

Saving redwoods has become everyone's business. On and on for years to come, anyone who wishes can by membership have a stake in it.

The
Redwood
Regions

Redwoods of Big Sur Country

To explore the redwoods of the coast, and if you are traveling from the south along Highway 1 from Morro Bay, you first come upon them at **Redwood Gulch** in southern Monterey County. But don't expect to find any cloudsweepers. The 500-mile long natural redwood range dribbles out just about here, for the less than 40-inch rainfall is insufficient to nurture the big ones. Still, it is worthwhile stopping at the sign to see the least of this noble race of trees and to know that they get bigger and taller the farther upcoast you go. Most of the north-facing slopes of the thirty or more canyons that plummet into the sea from the steep-faced Santa Lucias contain streams and redwoods. In some places trees grow almost to the water's edge. Many are on private property, some are inaccessible because of the terrain, but a few can be reached by rugged roads and trails.

Along **Willow Creek** you will find the largest of the southernmost groves. By driving in on the little dirt road 2.5 miles you come to the Willow Creek Campground sign, where you can park and take off on foot. It's 3 miles down into the redwood-lined canyon—a comfortable six-mile day's trek.

A few miles farther up the road, the redwoods become more accessible, such as those along **Mill Creek**. If you pick up the Nacimiento Road at the Kirk Creek Picnic Area, drive in less than a mile, and park, then you can hike for 2 miles through the redwoods.

Most southerly of the state redwood parks is the **Julia Pfeiffer-Burns State Park**, still largely undeveloped and much of it closed to the public. But it does offer some fine redwoods, a sheer waterfall where one of the several creeks tumble off a cliff into the sea, and

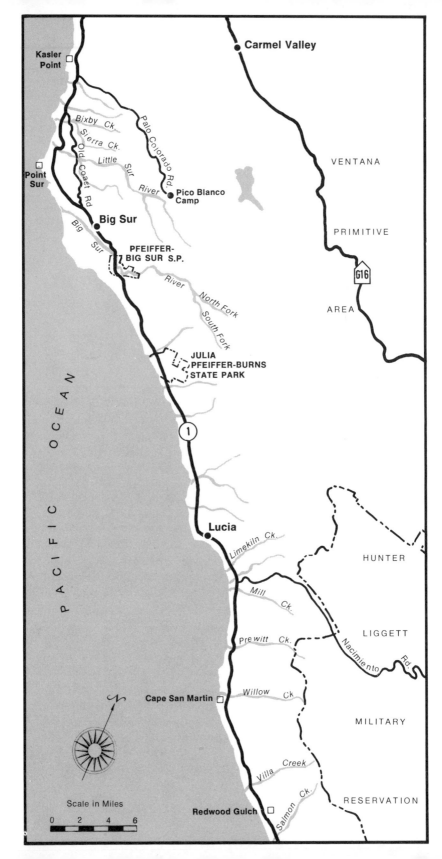

excellent overlooks from which to watch the Gray Whale migrations. The park, gifted to the state by Lathrop and Helen Brown to memorialize one of the Big Sur's earlyday pioneer women, covers nearly 1800 acres. Close to the highway are some picnic sites and a short trail. It's a good place to take a breather on the long winding road upcoast along the spectacular mountain front.

And there are other places, too, where travelers can pull out onto the many lofty vista points, for along here it is prudent not to try driving and gawking at the same time. From the overlooks you can see dark tree-lined canyons, some almost perpendicular, gashing the mountain front for miles in both directions. And with any luck—and some binoculars—there are sea otters to be discovered in the kelp beds far below.

About 35 miles south of Monterey, the Big Sur Highway leaves the cliffs and angling behind a ridge, descends into a narrow 10-mile long valley that emerges just below Point Sur. Nestled down in there is the **Pfeiffer-Big Sur State Park**, an 800-acre riverflat of meadow and redwood groves where the Big Sur River bursts from its gorge and bubbles peacefully through the park and on down to the sea. The park's name derives from the Pfeiffer family that settled here in 1869 and much later made substantial gifts of land to the state for park use. Here summers are utterly delightful and as a rule the winters are mild, the springtime enchanting. Camping is open year-round but subject to a 10-day limit from May through September. Reservations may be secured at Ticketron outlets or from the Department of Parks and Recreation, 1416 Ninth St. (P.O. Box 2390) Sacramento 95811. Some unreserved campsites are available on a first-come first-served basis. Understandably, the favored sites are in the redwoods along the river. Each has a table, stove, and cupboard with convenient water faucets, restrooms, hot showers and laundry facilities nearby. Although there are no trailer hookups, a few sites can accommodate 24-foot trailers and there is a trailer sanitation station. Lodge cabins are situated on a hill above the grocery, dining room, and gift shop—the center of activity along the Big Sur coast.

Sole entrance to the park is through the contact station near the Lodge. On one side of the river is the picnic area. One section of it can accommodate groups of up to 200 people. And there are three group campgrounds that in season (May 30-October 1) handle as many as 100. For them, write the Park Supervisor.

There is much to do at Big Sur. During the summer, rangers lead guided walks and bird watcher's hikes, provide nature exhibits to interpret the plant and animal life of the area, and conduct regular

Fishing in the Big Sur River may not be spectacular but small fry find it fun.

evening campfire programs. You will find plenty of opportunity to go off on your own along the easy self-guiding trail beside the river, up the shady path to Pfeiffer Falls or on the sunnier ones up the slopes on both sides of the park—even up the 3300-foot Mt. Manuel. If you are the hardy sort, try probing the Big Sur Gorge or hike the trails back into the vast Los Padres National Forest and the Ventana Wilderness Area east of the park. Then there's always trout and steelhead fishing in season and surf fishing south of the park at the mouth of Sycamore Canyon. Ask the rangers. They'll advise you. The Big Sur River, itself, is usually low enough in the summer for kiddie dunking and splashing.

All of this, together with its fascinating history and abundant wildlife, makes Pfeiffer-Big Sur State Park one of the most popular of coastal vacation spots. Here you won't be pestered by bears, just friendly raccoons, foxes, gray squirrels, skunks, opossums, and black-tailed deer. Varmints, such as lions, coyotes, and the belligerent wild boar, stay in the back country. Best to steer clear of the latter. They are huge and in no mood to put up with outlanders.

Where the Big Sur Valley begins to open out toward the sea at Point Sur is the recently opened **Andrew Molera State Park**. Although some redwoods grow here, this is more an area of open meadow, beach, rocky cliffs, and a lagoon at the rivermouth. It has proven excellent for varied wildlife-watching, both sea and land, as well as stream, rock, and surf fishing, but until facilities are provided, its 2000 acres must remain open for casual day use only.

Moving upcoast from Point Sur a few miles, you come to the famous Bixby Creek Bridge, one of the highest single span concrete arches in the world. If you have the yen now—and the time—for some backroad exploration of truly spectacular country, you can turn off on the **Old Coast Road**, which circles inland between the bridge and Big Sur Valley. If you relish a dramatic combination of forested canyon, the barren brow of a steep-sided mountain range facing the infinity of sea and sky—and are used to pitching, soaring auto trails—you would appreciate this one. All together it is a 10-mile experience never to be forgotten both as to viewing and driving although in dry weather only.

Turn off on the dirt road just north of the bridge, climb steeply a mile or so, then drop down into Bixby Creek, following on south for a couple of miles along Sierra Creek, all the while in a beautiful stand of redwoods. Climbing from here, you cross the grassy mountainsides and then wind down into a splendid 1200-acre redwood grove in the Little Sur River Valley, where there are many trees of fair size. All of this is restricted private property except for the Little Sur Trail, which starts along the road at the South Fork of the Little Sur and crosses privately owned lands for the first two miles before entering the Los Padres National Forest. It invites exploration of an area that was logged in the 1950's.

A long seven miles from the junction at the Bixby Creek Bridge, the Old Coast Road leaves the Little Sur River and the redwoods as well. After a number of passages over lofty ridges overlooking coastline and sea, it finally winds its circuitous way back to the Big Sur Highway between Point Sur and the state park.

About three miles north of the Bixby Creek Bridge, and if you have at least half a day for exploring off the beaten path, turn in at the signed **Palo Colorado Road**. Paved for a short distance, but very narrow, it will take you several miles through the heavily forested **Palo Colorado Canyon** of summer homes, some perched on stilts, and by dirt road across the open Las Piedras Ridge. Southward now, it winds and dips and finally drops into the Little Sur watershed, ending at the Pico Blanco Boy Scout Camp and the primitive Little Sur forest campground. Here a wooded trail leads up the Jackson Creek Canyon.

California's Central Coast

Lumbering in this area was heavy in the decades following California's Gold Rush, so aside from the groves of largest redwoods preserved for parks, most of the trees you see are second-growth. Yet this forest is exquisite by any standards. In the 60 to 125 years since their logging, the redwoods, through their own natural renewal, have grown big and tall. One has only to drive any road in the mountains of the San Francisco Peninsula to observe with wonder the amazing regeneration that followed such a ruthless cutting. Where once there was raw devastation on every slope and in every canyon, now stands a verdant redwood forest that all but hides the big telltale stumps.

Newest of the state redwood parks on the Central Coast is the **Forest of Nisene Marks** back of Aptos. Because it is still undeveloped and mostly roadless, you would be able to drive only short distances either along Aptos Creek or by Buzzard Lagoon Road in from Corralitos before having to take off on foot. From one road's end to the other, it's about 7.5 miles, some of it through brush and creek bottom and over the old railroad bed left from lumbering near the turn of the century. But the second-growth redwood is already 5 to 6 feet in diameter, and here and there are huge stumps and a few unusual giants, at the time of logging not considered perfect enough to bother with. Even by hiking downhill from the Corralitos end, the crossing should provide workout enough for the hardiest.

Highway 9 from Santa Cruz into the mountains leaves the sunlit city edge and at once plunges into the redwood-dark canyon of the San Lorenzo River. It may seem like a noonday passing through the doorway of a dimly-lit chapel so quickly and pleasantly is the transition made. And for the next six miles the road will take you in dense shade around a succession of curves until near Felton you come upon an impressive redwood log sign on your right—**Henry Cowell Redwoods State Park.** Without question, Redwood Grove, the hub of this park is one of the really magnificent groups of the entire central coast redwood realm. Not quite as tall nor as big as those of the northern

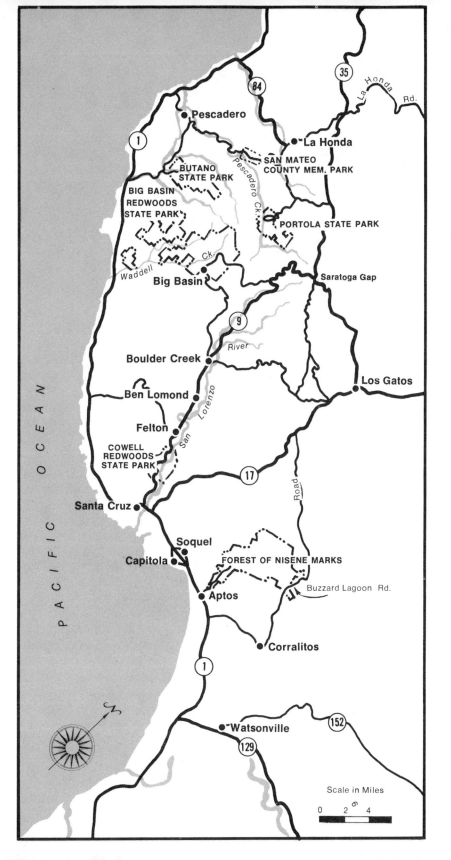

The Giant: Henry Cowell Redwoods State Park in the Santa Cruz Mountains: circumference 51 feet, height 285 feet.

counties, they are nevertheless unique and stately enough for anyone. The mile-long self-guided Redwood Grove Trail leads past one splendid giant after another, each indicated on the guide sheet you can pick up at the entrance station. On this easy and altogether pleasant loop walk, you will see the 285-foot Giant, the well-named Neckbreaker, the big crater, the Fremont Tree, the Burl Tree, and the Association Group besides many others. And, where the path begins and ends, you are bound to enjoy the Exhibit Shelter with its graphic interpretation of the park's wonders.

Henry Cowell Redwoods provides a picnic area near the grove overlooking the river, and a snack bar and gift shop. The Graham Hill Campground unit, which can accommodate trailers up to 36 feet, is a short distance away on the Graham Hill Road. Its campsites and facilities are typical of most throughout the coastal state parks, only this particular area is in a stand of Ponderosa pines, usually found much farther inland and at higher, drier elevations.

Fifteen miles of hiking and riding trails lead to outlying semi-wilderness areas. Running hourly alongside one edge of the park and up through the redwood forest to the top of Bear Mountain puffs the steam locomotive and cars of the Roaring Camp and Big Trees Railroad. One of the few narrow gauge excursion trains operating in the West, it is a popular spot indeed.

Big Basin Redwoods State Park, California's first state park, is also one of the most popular. Its convenient geographical location 24 miles upcanyon from Santa Cruz and 67 miles south of San Francisco via the Skyline Boulevard probably accounts for its heavy usage. From Henry Cowell Redwoods and Felton, just follow Highway 9 to Boulder Creek's main intersection, then turn left on Highway 236 up Boulder Creek Canyon, climbing over the sunny-meadowed rim and down into the big grove in the heart of the park at the bottom of the Basin. The drive itself is a joy if one moves at a leisurely pace, for this two-lane winding road is no freeway and there is much to see en route—cabins, private parks, several small and picturesque towns.

Entering from upper Highway 9 on the San Francisco side (but please not in trailers and such) you are treated to some tiered mountain vistas and an open jackpine and madrone forest while twisting and looping your way 8 miles down into the shady magnificence of Park Center with its full-round log ranger station at 1000-feet elevation —and all around you, huge, towering redwoods.

Big Basin has some of the mightiest giants south of the Bay Area. Be sure to stroll the level Redwood Trail around the main grove to see the massive Father of the Forest, the Animal Tree, the Chimney

Tree, the Mother Tree, and many others.

Then visit the Nature Lodge. There, together with displays of redwood growth and mounted specimens of the Big Basin birds and other wildlife, you will find some really graphic exhibits depicting the park's topography, geology, history, and earlyday lumbering techniques.

Adjacent is a gift shop and grocery and nearby a snack bar. Scenic camp and picnic sites are usually available except during the seasonal rush and on weekends, and of a summer you will have well-attended evening campfires to enjoy. Don't be afraid to take off on your own along the many signed trails within the nearly 12,000 acres. Rangers at Park Headquarters will provide a trail map and excellent advice and direction. One hiking trail goes 23 miles to Castle Rock State Park and another to a beautiful waterfall. Horsebackers have 15 miles of trail, too.

Camping has to be limited to 15 days in the 235-family sites. The group area can accommodate up to 200 people. All are by reservation. Some have sufficient room for small recreational vehicles, and although there are no trailer hookups, one campground has a trailer sanitation station.

In addition to all the human activity in Big Basin during the summer are the comings and goings of the many birds and animals who call the park and its environs home. Deer and squirrels, quite tame, are seen around the central area along with the sassy Stellar jay and others of its kind. Raccoons come visiting at night. Seen less often are skunks, foxes, opossums, and coyotes. No bears or lions will be there to bother you.

In the early summer, azaleas bloom fragrantly; in the middle and later summer, huckleberries are ripe for picking.

As in all state parks: a camping fee; pets on leash not exceeding six feet, enclosed in vehicle or tent at night; and for dogs, a license and proof of rabies innoculation.

Portola State Park, the first camping park south of San Francisco, is in a shady natural bowl nestled in the western side of the city's mountainous peninsula and reached via the Skyline Boulevard, Highway 35, then west down Alpine Road. Secluded among tall Douglas fir and groves of second-growth redwoods, Portola has excellent family and group camp and picnic sites in big tree groves. Because of its proximity to the Sunday picnicking population centers of the Bay Area, it is usually a busy place on weekends.

Pescadero Creek runs through the park, providing some trout fishing opportunities, and there are 14 miles of hiking trails, some to

Visitors look small, indeed, alongside the giants in Big Basin.

*Everyone enjoys the friendly deer in the meadow
and strolling around Park Center and the
campground at Big Basin.*

higher, sunnier elevations and mostly over rugged terrain. These you may like to explore with the park naturalist or to enjoy them and the Sequoia Self-Guiding Nature Trail and its Chimney Tree on your own. If you want to see the finest of the redwoods in the groves above Peters and Pescadero Creeks, follow the Iverson Trail, starting behind the Park Visitor Center.

In the cool, sometimes foggy evenings, rangers conducting campfire programs will tell you about the area's nature lore, its fascinating history, and really unique geology.

The **Butano State Park** is reached by coastal Highway 1 north of Santa Cruz. From the Pescadero turnoff, take the Cloverdale Road several miles into the western slope of the mountains. There you find a dense forest of both mature and second-growth redwoods and Douglas fir with Little Butano Creek running through it. Still under development, the park nevertheless provides 40 improved campsites and a number of "walk-in" ones not far away. Rangers are there to lead

*Coons come begging, borrowing, or stealing in
most coastal redwood parks—much to the delight of
campers—sometimes even by day.*

nature walks and weekend campfire programs and to generally help
you to enjoy and appreciate the restful quiet of this remote redwood
forest. Since the Butano falls heir to some overflow from the other
peninsula mountain parks, reservations are advisable during the summer for the 15-day-limit campsites.

San Mateo County Memorial Park you can reach from the
Skyline 7 miles north of the Portola State Park turnoff. Take the La
Honda Road, then just beyond La Honda, bend southward on Pesca-
dero Road.

The park is a beautiful stand of redwoods that survived the
tanoak logging early in the century. It has well developed facilities for
camping, picnicking, hiking, and offers ample opportunity for nature
study. If you'd like to strike out by yourself, ask at the entrance station
for a trail guide and booklet identifying the park plants and wildlife.
Evening campfires can enlighten and entertain you further—and then
there's the swimmin' hole where the creek has been dammed.

Try not to miss the tiny park a few miles farther on Skyline Boulevard where stands the craggy **Methuselah Tree.** Its great trunk knotted with burls measures 14 feet in diameter above the burls, and while the tree is a scant 137 feet high, it doesn't taper noticeably. Until broken off in a storm, this old giant was once nearly a hundred feet taller. It takes incredible endurance to have survived the violence of the elements through the centuries.

Redwoods North of the Bay

What a pity that all of us arrived in California too late to enjoy the magnificent redwood forests once covering the hills around San Francisco Bay before the Gold Rush—indeed before 1834 and California's first water-powered sawmill near Santa Rosa; before 1843 and the first steam-powered sawmill near Bodega Bay. Some stands on the East Bay hills were tall and distinctive enough to have served as landmarks for mariners entering the Golden Gate. But because they were close to the young, rapidly-growing city across the bay, these giants were among the first to go. Still, with the amazing vitality of their kind, they rejuvenated themselves through their stump sprouts, and began once again to reach for the sky.

Today, over a century later, their tall-tree stands spread across the brow of the East Bay hills and crowd down into residential Oakland and Berkeley. In the Redwood Regional Park above Oakland you will find the best of them. The access road winds through several groves that nestle picnic sites, and the two-mile trail, which starts at the end of the road and leads up a redwood-lined canyon, is well worth seeing.

Mount Tamalpais, overlooking both ocean and bay is a century-long hikers delight. In the first place, much of its 200 miles of signed trail are in the view-in-a-million category, for even though the mountain rises only 2600 feet, it provides "the works" for Bay Area residents hungry for quiet and an acute need to see out.

Many miles of the trail lying within the 5000-acre **Mount Tamalpais State Park**'s western slope tie in with the trails of Muir Woods National Monument, pocketed in and encircled by the park at the mountain's seaward base. Walk-in camping is provided at Pan Toll and Bootjack and two group areas at the Alice Eastwood Camp—but reservations are necessary. Picnic sites are available, too. For real

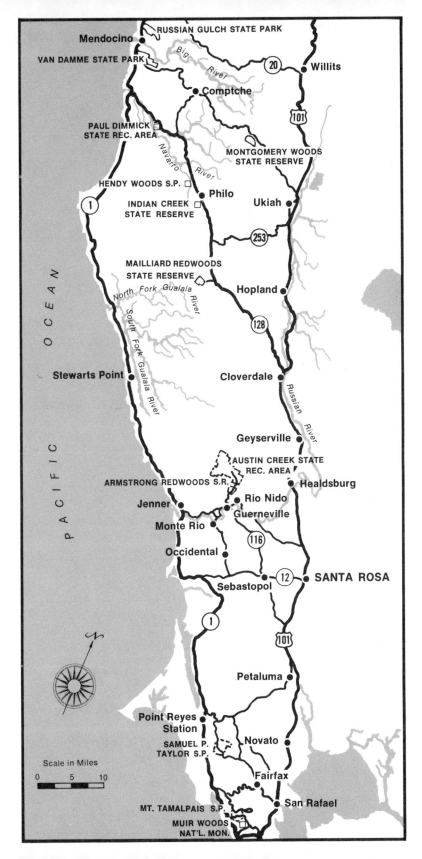

Redwood Regional Park above Oakland
is a popular mecca for picnickers.

escape, though, hike down the Steep Ravine Trail, a shady wilderness canyon of redwoods and ferns following the cascading Webb Creek from the Matt Davis Trail in Bootjack Camp. In there you can revel in the little stream and the feeling of being away from everyone. Also try the fire road between the Alice Eastwood group campground and Muir Woods as well as Redwood Creek downstream from Bootjack.

Best access to the redwoods of "Mt. Tam" is via State Highway 1 to Panoramic Highway, then ascending the mountain about five miles from Mill Valley to the state park headquarters at Pan Toll. The road is narrow and winding and definitely not for sightseeing while at the wheel. But whether viewing the world from the summit or hiking down one of the redwood canyons, you are bound to feel liberated from everyday life.

Only a few miles from the heavily congested Bay Area is **Muir Woods National Monument.** Being one of the really verdant canyons of redwoods and easily accessible, it enjoys enormous popularity. Reached from the Redwood Highway U.S. 101 north of the Golden

Gate, thence from Panoramic Highway by both car and tour bus, visitor attendance is nothing less than phenomenal. A dense stand of towering redwoods, Douglas fir, tanoak, bay, and numerous streamside broadleaf trees densely shade the central grove, well floored with ferns and other ground cover. Through it flows Redwood Creek, a mere trickle in the summer, a bouldery uphill swimway for salmon and steelhead when swollen with winter rains. Nix on fishing, though—not within the monument.

Alongside the stream and up to the high points go six miles of trail that beckon to a wide variety of scenery and experience—some lead to breathtaking overlooks, others such as the main trail into the redwoods, to Cathedral and Bohemian Groves. If it is just an easy stroll you'd like, sample the Nature Trail. The trees and shrubs are signed for identification, and even on that short loop it is possible to see the more mobile inhabitants of this peaceful glen—a blacktailed deer, some chipmunks, perhaps near sundown when the monument closes, a raccoon out on his evening search for crawdads in the creek.

Muir Woods does not provide for picnicking or camping, but all humanity seems to wind up there sooner or later. Go during the week if possible and avoid the crowds. While there, take a look at the albino redwood shoots and the Dawn redwood and the memorial plaque honoring William Kent, who bought this place to be preserved as the country's first national monument. Best of all, though, you'll probably enjoy simply being there, for Muir Woods has a restful beauty all its own.

Scarcely an hour's ride from the Golden Gate by way of the Francis Drake Boulevard (in from #101 at San Rafael) is **Samuel P. Taylor State Park**, a beautifully wooded area of 2600 acres. Here, typically, the redwood groves populate the ferned canyon floor and the north-facing slopes. Inviting camp and picnic sites set on lush groundcover and in cool shade attract steel-and-concrete weary Bay Area folk, who like to drive there on weekends, either for overnight in one of the quiet campsites or for a day's outing and barbecue. Only small trailers requiring no electric, water, or sewer hookups can be accommodated, but there'll be a special spot waiting should you come bicycling or backpacking. And anyone using the State Hiking and Riding Trails is certain to appreciate Devils Gulch Camp with its corral, water troughs, and hitching racks. Be sure, though, to make reservations well in advance for this and the group camp.

To add to your pleasure are many miles of trail to a variety of points, a short nature trail, and innumerable places in the creek for wading and swimming. Of interest, too, is the history of this section

*Between 1907 and 1930 Muir Woods was the lower
terminus of the Mt. Tamalpais and Muir Woods
Railway. Today it is a quiet grove of paths winding
among the giant redwoods.*

—the story of Samuel P. Taylor's fortunes in the Gold Rush, what he did with his gold dust, how he gave name to this beautiful canyon and rolling hills by building here the first papermill in the West. The fascinating yarn is told in the leaflet handed out at the gate.

Many visitors like to get double their money's worth by approaching Samuel P. Taylor from the bay and leaving oceanward by taking State Highway 1 through Olema so they can enjoy the exciting coastline, its beaches and headlands, especially the Bolinas Lagoon, the Audubon Ranch, and the Pt. Reyes National Seashore just eight miles to the north.

The Russian River, "San Francisco's Playground," has long been the objective of city vacationers heading for the magic combination of river and tall timber. On the riverside roads between the Redwood Highway at Santa Rosa or Healdsburg and Jenner near where the Russian empties into the sea, you'll find all kinds of resorts set in the deep shade of second-growth redwoods. The little village of Guerneville (pronounced Gurn'-ville) is the heart of the Russian River country and its business center. During the warm months it becomes a beehive of activity—all contributing to sunbathing on sandy beaches and water sports of every sort on the river; picnicking and camping, partying and relaxing at the myriad of cabins tucked in among the tall redwoods. The picturesque resort communities of Rio Nido and Monte Rio add to the scene, and the Russian River itself has its day between November and February, when steelhead swarm upstream and fishermen swarm to its banks, rod and reel in hand. A far cry, all of this, from the days before, during, and after the Gold Rush that saw the giant forests along here logged off to build San Francisco into a teeming young city.

Turning in from Guerneville, move north a couple of miles to **Armstrong Redwoods State Reserve**, the only state preserve on the Russian River with camping and day-use facilities. This place has its full share of devotees—a yearly head-count of over 200,000—although to some visitors the well watered and densely forested central grove is dark enough to be forbidding.

After a walk around the self-guiding nature trail and a look at some of the giants, such as the 310-foot Parson Jones Tree, why not see if there isn't something going on at the Redwood Forest Theater, a natural amphitheater. During the summer, dramatic and musical productions are staged here—to say nothing of countless outdoor weddings. On beyond the nature trail and Luther Burbank Circle you will find the park's camping and picnicking areas.

Leaving them behind, you come to the much larger and sunnier

Throngs of vacationists journey to the famed Russian River each year to enjoy its sand beaches and cool waters.

Austin Creek State Recreation Area, a grassy swale of rolling mountains, alder-lined canyons, several creeks and many springs. Hikers and horseback riders, especially, appreciate the remote roominess of this area with its Horse Haven campground, improved family campsites, and its inaccessibility to larger recreational vehicles.

Armstrong Redwoods should be of interest to history buffs who would like to learn about the determined and successful efforts of earlyday settler Colonel James B. Armstrong to preserve his valley of really magnificent giants for future enjoyment.

One cannot think of the Redwood Empire without also thinking of **Highway 1 North**—north, that is, from San Francisco, along spectacular bluffs and around deep-set coves, past Point Reyes and its tall lighthouse, past Tomales Bay and Bodega Head to the mouth of the Russian River; then on upcoast for another 145 miles before climbing over the mountains and hooking into the Redwood Highway at Leggett Valley near Standish-Hickey and Smithe groves. This has always been one of the least known and most dramatic stretches of California.

It was here in the Bodega Bay area in the early 1800's that both Russians and Yankees hunted the sea otter almost to extinction and left their marks on the landscape in name and structure. Fort Ross, now a state historical monument, was from 1811 to 1841 a high stockade protecting some sixty-odd rough-hewn buildings of the Russian settlement. By contrast, the little lumber villages of white clapboard houses strung along the seaside cliffs, are redolent of the unmistakable flavor of New England.

Most travelers like to stop at historic Fort Ross and go into the Orthodox chapel, the Commander's quarters and the stockade blockhouses (all solid redwood hewn from the forests climbing the hills behind the old fort) before moving on up the northwesterly-trending coastline.

Beyond there, one after another, promontories jut out into the sea, coves retreat into the lee of sheltering cliffs, and trestles cross high over gulches floored by streams emptying into the surf. Here and there, sometimes boldly facing storm and saltspray, sometimes tucked into more protected spots, stand what remains of once thriving lumber towns, mill sites, and ancient landings in the dogholes where long ago coastwise vessels put in to take on cargo and waddle out, their loaded decks almost awash. Each settlement depended upon the redwood forests that rose tall and dark at its back and the whims of wind and tide against the cliffs out front. Stewart's Point, Gualala, Point Arena, Manchester, Greenwood, Elk, Albion, Little River, Mendocino, Casper, Noyo, Fort Bragg, Westport—they're all there, more or less, between the redwoods and the sea, still colored by history roughly and vigorously lived. Of such is Highway 1 North—dynamic, fascinating, unforgettable.

Mailliard Redwoods State Park, a short distance in from Highway 128 on an unsigned county road about twenty miles west of Cloverdale, still remains mostly undeveloped. The small stand of redwoods named for John Ward Mailliard, a conservationist, is beautiful, the grove remote and peaceful with a tiny creek, actually the headwaters of the Garcia River, running through it. Fishing is prohibited, though, because the stream is a spawning grounds for salmon and steelhead. There are a few picnic tables, but the reserve is without restrooms and therefore Off Limits to camping.

Very much the same can be said for **Indian Creek State Reserve**, a small redwood rest stop a dozen miles or so farther west along Highway 128. A good place for a stretch, this, and a spot of coffee out of the old thermos. Perhaps even a casual picnic.

Something else again is **Hendy Woods State Park**, three miles beyond Philo on the road to Elk. It lies in a flat valley less than a mile off the highway. As yet not well publicized—but certainly one of the really fine groves of redwoods in this entire area—it is a place to go to escape the crush. Campsites are usually available in the two campgrounds, both in mixed redwood and Douglas fir stands; and the picnic sites are scenically located along the Navarro River, where sunbathing and dunking is a delight. Unimproved trails loop through Little Hendy and Big Hendy Groves of big trees that rise as high as 250 feet and have diameters up to 17 feet. A good place for leisurely walks and poking around to find the unusual giants—the fire-scarred ones and those that have adjusted in different ways to the violence of Nature, and are renewing themselves.

For anyone seeking to return to relatively simple outdoorsmanship in a setting of towering forest and a thick growth of ferns and a lazy river, Hendy has much to offer. Summers tend to be warm, winters sopping wet, spring and autumn perfect—with the added joy of fall and winter salmon and steelhead fishing between the park and the ocean. Nature walks are conducted on Saturday mornings during the summer. Altogether, youngsters as well as adults will love Hendy Woods.

Back again on Highway 128, you come to the dense second-growth redwoods of tiny **Paul M. Dimmick Wayside Camp** along the Navarro River. Here are beautiful camp and picnic sites, and being a bit inland from the summer fogs, the vacation season temperatures are pleasant both for river play and the seasonal salmon and steelhead fishing. A good spot to headquarter for the leisurely exploration and enjoyment of the river and the Mendocino coast beckoning just eight miles away.

Adjoining Dimmick are parking nooks for recreational vehicles, bicyclists and foot travelers, which have been provided by the Masonite Company on their extensive lands.

About 15 miles west of Ukiah on the Comptche-Ukiah Road and approximately 2 miles beyond Orrs Hot Springs you will find **Montgomery Woods State Reserve** at the headwaters of Big River. It is a walk-in stand of big stately redwoods with a loop trail and some commemorative groves. But the unimproved road leading to it is so long and winding that visitation here is sparse. As yet the park remains undeveloped, but does offer some unusually fine redwoods and a mass of woodwardia ferns well worth the grind of getting to them.

On now to the sea and the happy combination of rugged coastline, the cool damp of Little River's fern-lined canyon opening out into a cove, and wooded camp and picnic sites at **Van Damme State Park**.

A natural amphitheatre located under towering redwoods in Armstrong Redwood State Recreation area near Guerneville, Sonoma County, seats 2000 people for outdoor concerts, church services and weddings.

The glassy waters of the Navarro River flow quietly
past the Dimmick campground.

The redwoods in this steep-sided canyon three miles south of Mendocino are second-growth among red alders mixed with an outstanding rain forest population of all kinds of ferns and their companion plants. Because of the park's mild temperatures and its shelter from ocean winds, it attracts inland valley residents fleeing the heat.

During the Civil War this canyon mouth was the site of a sawmill, and Little River, a dammed up millpond. Settlers from New England even built their own lumber schooners there on the north side of the cove. Charles Van Damme, who gave name to this charming park, was born at Little River, lived to become a San Francisco ferryboat tycoon, and returned to buy his home place and open it to the public. After his death in 1934, the family gave what became the nucleus of the present park.

The short upcanyon road follows an old skid road. The dam is gone but trails lead from the canyon road. One of these, which is self-guiding, will take you to the ancient Pygmy Forest in the southeastern section of the park—a fascinating area of mature, cone-bearing pines and cypress only a few feet high and probably a hundred years old, stunted because of unusual acid soil conditions. This unique forest can also be reached by car from the coast just north of the post office and store.

Cold ocean water at the cove makes swimming, except for Eskimos, quite undesirable, but the pebbled sands invite fire-ring picnicking or just beachcombing. As you may expect, tidepools are nearby. Because these have been repeatedly stripped of their marine life, visitors have been asked to merely peek and watch, and leave as-is so life there can continue. Popular in the same and other rocky areas are fishing and skindiving for abalone.

On up the spectacular Mendocino coast, one passes Little River Inn, so well reflecting the New England character of the earlyday settlers, as does picturesque **Mendocino** atop a wave-battered headland farther on. This village, once a lumber port and now an artist colony, is a must for anyone with nostalgia for our colorful coastline past.

Just north of there lies **Russian Gulch State Park**. It extends out onto a jagged promontory, wave-cut into lofty view points, coves, and sandy beaches—prime favorites of sunbathers and rock fishermen and skindivers exploring underwater or searching for abalone. Out there also is a 200-foot long sea tunnel, partially collapsed, that has become a big, flower-encircled blowhole called the Devil's Punch Bowl. Although it doesn't actually blow, the sea surges through it with the surf and tide.

The gulch, itself, several miles long, is well forested with second-growth redwood, Douglas fir, and their usual associates, including a varied and lush growth of berry bushes, azalea, and rhododendron. Russian Gulch Creek waters the canyon floor.

In this protected setting are a number of campsites, open from March 15 to November, some available to trailers of under 20 feet. Toward its mouth, the creek broadens and shallows, providing a delightful splashing place for youngsters. A group campground and recreation hall add to the park's facilities. Picnic sites in the Bishop pines out on the headland and fire rings on the beach are open year round.

At the inland end of the narrow canyon road and bicycle path along the creek, you'll find the start of the 3½-mile Falls Loop Trail to the 52-foot high waterfalls. Other trails lead to the Pygmy Forest and out around the headlands to the Devil's Punch Bowl.

Wildlife in this scenic coastal park is varied and quite numerous, especially the birdlife along the shore. Raccoons, chipmunks, deer and fox—and even a bobcat now and then—make their appearance to

Peaceful and picturesque, the Redwood Empire
town of Mendocino, Mendocino County, perches
on a bluff overlooking the Pacific Ocean.

the delight of visitors. In the creek you'll discover trout for seasonal catching, but the salmon and steelhead are a definite No-No, for these are spawning waters. Small boats may be carried across the beach and launched, although offshore fishing here is risky. A few miles upcoast, Noyo has facilities for large craft and there are also party fishing boats at several villages not far away.

Travelers driving on north over the coast highway as far as the photogenic fishing village of Noyo or on to the little town of Fort Bragg would miss an exciting fun experience if they did not ride one of the **California Western Railroad's Skunks** from Fort Bragg across the mountains to Willits on the Redwood Highway. More than just train buffs love this two-hour ride through the redwood wilderness, either by the single diesel-car Skunk or the steam locomotive Super Skunk pulling brightly colored passenger cars.

On the 40 miles of multiple twists and turns, the Skunks cross

Noyo Harbor–nerve center of Mendocino County's commercial sea-going fleet. Visitors tour the packing houses and sports fishermen go after salmon and albacore.

44 bridges and trestles and chug through two tunnels. The course is so winding that in one place, known as the Bowknot, they switch back and forth 8½ miles while actually moving onward just a mile and a half.

Part way across and deep in the redwood forest, the engineer calls a rest stop. While the Super Skunk takes on water for the crooked climb toward Willits, passengers may get off, enjoy refreshments at the stand there, take pictures, and perhaps explore a bit. And because it is all very informal, other short stops are often made enroute to observe a bear or deer and to deliver groceries and mail to the few inhabitants of this remote hinterland.

Skunks make the crossing and back every day from late May until after Labor Day, but because the trips are in great demand, be sure to obtain a schedule and reservations well ahead of your arrival. Overnight accommodations in Fort Bragg are ample. An early morning departure from the depot and a mid or late afternoon return is the

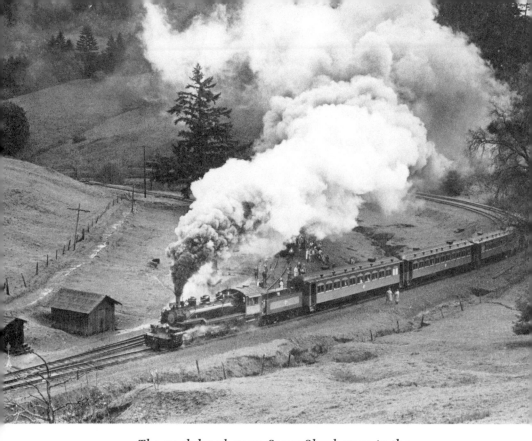

*The much-loved steam Super Skunk stops in the
back country to have its picture taken and to give
the passengers a breather.*

custom. Write California Western Railroad, Box 907-B, Fort Bragg
95437.

Oh yes—you wondered how in the world a train was named
Skunk? Back in 1925 the first rail passenger service, a gasoline-
powered car, had the natives holding their noses. Such stinky fumes
they simply were not accustomed to in their rain and ocean-washed air,
so they began referring to their transportation system as you-know-
what. And so it has remained.

While in Fort Bragg you might like to take a free guided tour
through the Union Lumber Company mill there, one of the big ones,
to see how huge logs are handled from Millpond to drying yards. It is
well worthwhile, noisy, and fascinating.

Redwoods of Eel River Country

The Branscomb Road west of Laytonville on the Redwood Highway, U.S. 101, is only a partially paved road, and about 13 miles out is **Admiral William Standley State Recreation Area**. Small and still undeveloped, it consists of little more than a beautiful stand of redwoods with a stream flowing through it, beside which you may spread your red-checked tablecloth and picnic in absolute simplicity.

Back on the Redwood Highway, a traveler can move on north through the famous Redwood Empire, coming first to the **Standish-Hickey State Recreation Area** just beyond Leggett. Here second-growth redwoods and big Douglas firs make a cozy place for picnickers to spend the day, for campers an enjoyable setting in generally pleasant summer weather. Nicely situated along the South Fork of the Eel River, the park offers a variety of campgrounds: two older ones near the highway, one with a campfire circle and picnic area; the third on the slopes across the river in a stand of small redwoods. There is a big tree, though, about a mile away by a trail that also goes to a waterfall. The Captain Miles Standish Tree, 225 feet tall, rises in dramatic majesty out of an area of second-growth regenerating from a 1945 fire. It was named for the well-remembered personage of America's early history, and ancestor of the donors of this parkland to the California State Park System.

A steep path descends to the river, its cool waters ideal for both good swimmers and youngsters. Another trail, the Mill Creek Loop, five miles long and extremely rugged, sweeps southward to a lofty viewpoint.

A few miles north of Standish-Hickey and rounding a down-curve, you suddenly come upon **Smithe Redwoods State Reserve**, a stately grove of big trees between the highway and the Eel River. Once it was Lane's Redwood Flat, a private resort. Now, minus all commercialism it stands quietly in its own natural splendor. Restrooms are the only facility, but here is a fine level place to stop and work kinks out of legs while strolling among some really impressive old giants.

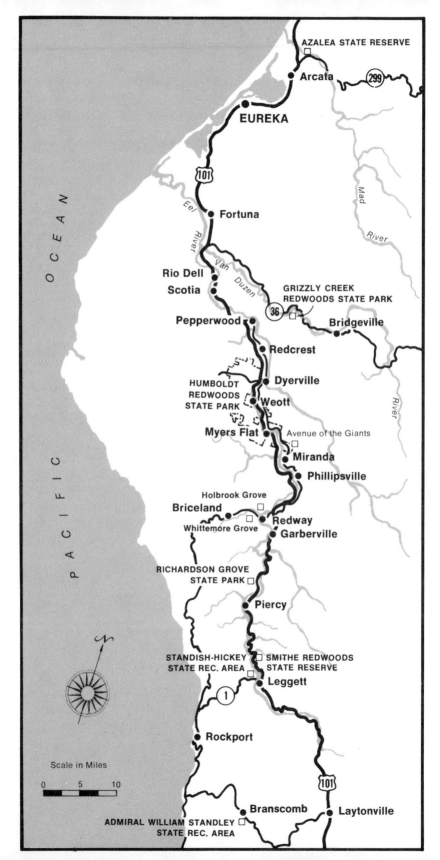

AZALEA STATE RESERVE

Arcata

(299)

EUREKA

101

Eel River

Fortuna

Van Duzen

Rio Dell

Scotia

GRIZZLY CREEK
REDWOODS STATE PARK

Pepperwood

(36)

Bridgeville

Redcrest

HUMBOLDT
REDWOODS
STATE PARK

Dyerville

Weott

Myers Flat

Avenue of the Giants

OCEAN

Miranda

Phillipsville

Holbrook Grove

Briceland

Whittemore Grove

Redway

Garberville

RICHARDSON GROVE
STATE PARK

PACIFIC

Piercy

STANDISH-HICKEY
STATE REC. AREA

SMITHE REDWOODS
STATE RESERVE

Leggett

1

Rockport

Scale in Miles

0   5   10

101

Branscomb

Laytonville

ADMIRAL WILLIAM STANDLEY
STATE REC. AREA

Mad River

River

And if the edge of the grove along the riverbank is too much to leave right away, why not picnic informally or even remain long enough to catch a fish or two? Certainly the grove warrants a stopover of some kind, if only to stand and gaze upwards in awe.

After crossing the Humboldt County line and with nine miles yet to go before entering little Garberville, the principal business, service, and supply town of the area, the highway emerges from redwoods and out onto a short stretch of river vista. Then it plunges into the deep shade of **Richardson Grove State Park**. Almost as if passing into another world, most travelers automatically slow in surprise.

Lining both sides of the highway are huge old-growth redwoods that shelter enticing picnic sites along the river. The main area, itself, which the highway bisects, is as attractive a forest center as any to be found in the entire Redwood Empire. Be sure to park, visit the concession, and walk the self-guiding Redwood Trail of unusual exhibits, one of the best in redwood country. One of these, a fallen giant, reveals how the tree had adapted after each of seven separate floods that had roared through the flat during its lifetime.

For many years Richardson Grove, named for a former governor, has been a favorite of vacationing families. Most of the old campsites along the river, however, were "put to bed" some time ago; this to save the main grove from further trampling by the more than half a million visitors yearly who have almost loved it to death. But there are three varied campgrounds for the fifteen-day limit permitted—the Madrone and Huckleberry campgrounds on the slope above the center, and the Oak Flat Campground across the river.

Besides the several easy paths through the towering redwoods of the flat, all kinds of trails spread out over the area, some leading through woodlands and out to ridges, where a hiker can go alone or on one of the daily nature walks.

In the mild summertime, swimming in the river and sunbathing on the beach coaxes numerous visitors into the open, and at night during the vacation months, campfires draw the overnighters together for singing and the rangers' talks and slides on local history and nature lore.

The park is year round. Even in the cold rainy winters, visitors are impelled to stop in the grandeur of this grove to saunter among the giants. Many fishermen come here to try the river for silver and king salmon and steelhead. Richardson Grove is one of the redwood parks best remembered of all those along the famed Redwood Highway.

About four miles to the north the traveler rounds a turn and

Framed in big trees above, is one of the more than 150 campsites at Standish Hickey State Park in Northern Mendocino County.

finds stretched out ahead what looks like a glassy lake where a river ought to be—**Benbow Lake State Recreation Area**. And situated on a grassy hill above the water, overlooking it, stands picturesque Benbow Inn, long a popular hostelry.

Actually the lake is a lake and yet a river, the Eel, impounded by the temporary Benbow Dam, which is usually installed about the end of May and removed after Labor Day. So if it's a swim or merely a sunning you'd like and a bite of lunch, pull off to the nicely-grassed picnic grounds along the shore for an hour or a day. You could camp in the woods across the river if you like a simple campground. Rackety powerboats and water skiing are taboo here, so this jewel of a spot is great for canoes and kayaks which glide through the crystal clear reflections on the waters of the lake.

Largest of all of redwood country's parks, and one of the most magnificent, is the 40-mile long, 43,000-acre **Humboldt Redwoods State Park** in the heart of the Redwood Empire. In it are some of the finest of the coastal old-growth, added section by section, grove by grove, as the Save-the-Redwoods League and the state could find the purchase money. Through the length of it runs the Avenue of the Giants Parkway. Little villages catering to the tourists dot the route such as Phillipsville, Miranda, Myers Flat, Weott, Redcrest, and Pepperwood.

Approaching from the south, you come upon the first unit of Humboldt Redwoods at Whittemore Grove, a few miles west of Garberville and Redway on the Briceland Road. It lies on the other side of the Eel River's South Fork, which you will be following for some time as soon as you back up to Redway and head north a couple of miles, first passing through Holbrook Grove. Both Whittemore and Holbrook groves offer cool shade when most needed as well as short walks, informal picnicking, and in places, access to the river. The big delights along the stream are the numerous places where a vacationer can enjoy both the riverside groves of big trees and the pebbly beaches and water holes that border them. Swimming and innertube floating in placid water, either deep or shallow, fishing in all seasons (especially silver and king salmon and steelhead in fall and winter) sunbathing and beach or grove picnicking are there to be chosen from, or all of it sampled.

Back on U.S. 101 and after three miles, turn from the rush-rush multi-lane freeway onto the two-lane Old Redwood Highway, which at Miranda becomes the 33-mile long **Avenue of the Giants Parkway.** There the speed limit is low and most of the trees over 300 feet high. For many of the next 40 miles venerable giants, centuries old, line both sides of this quiet road and reach for the clouds. In here it's like driving through a narrow but living gorge, where sunlight is able to touch the pavement and the groundcover of oxalis, ferns, and a myriad of wildflowers and flowering shrubs only on rare occassions when the sun, at its zenith, happens to filter through the lofty foliage in misty shafts.

Clear to **Dyerville Flat**, the road meanders along the east side of the South Fork, much of the distance past one splendid grove after another and once in a while a sunny meadow. Along the way, the traveler finds turnouts where some parking is available and the primeval groves of almost pure redwood invite casual picnicking and exploration. Some even have short loop trails or little dirt roads leading to the river. Many of the 70 memorial groves honor individuals or the organizations that helped preserve them. Just to mention a few of the dedicated units: between Phillipsville and nearby Franklin K. Lane Grove and Dyerville Flat, where the South and main forks of the Eel merge, you find the **Children's Forest** and the **Garden Club of America** groves in tranquil solitude on the west side of the river; **Williams Grove**, largest of the picnic areas; **Hidden Springs** and the **Burlington Campground**, both with excellent facilities and activities; the **Federated Women's Club Grove**; just beyond, the **Founders Grove**, named for the first leaders of the Save-the-Redwoods League. Well worth a slight sashay to the parking area, it offers an easy self-guided nature trail through the grove's unusually tall and impressive redwoods. One of them was for years designated the world's tallest tree—364 feet—until the top shattered off in a 1958 storm and somewhat later several 367-foot giants were discovered on Redwood Creek farther north. Nevertheless, the Dyerville Giant soars 358 feet into the sky and those around it rise almost as high.

At the other end of the Dyerville Bridge, just beyond the Founders Grove, be sure to turn coastward under the freeway on the Honeydew Road and into the splendid **Rockefeller Forest**. There alongside Bull Creek, you will be treated to what has been ably described as the grandest redwood grove of all. It is not quite the stand it was before the devastating floods of 1955 and 1964 but even so, there are more than 700 acres of ancient giants guaranteed to dwarf any man gazing up at them.

Parking at **Bull Creek Flat**, about five miles in from the bridge, the visitor finds a short trail to the 359-foot tallest tree in the Rockefeller Forest. And by footbridge he can cross the creek and walk a level trail to the spectacular Big Tree and the Flatiron Tree, which is 7.5 feet in diameter at the braced side of the giant and 17.5 feet on the opposite side. Deep in this forest—or any of the others along the day's route

*Tallest One-Room House In The World is in Mendocino
County near Piercy. Tree measures 101½ feet in circumference
at its base, is 250 feet tall and is estimated 2000 years old.
Long ago it was gutted by fire, leaving a cavity 50 feet high
and making a room 21 x 27 feet.*

Redwoods of Eel River Country   **93**

This great Chandelier Tree at Underwood Park in Mendocino County is pierced by a 7-foot hole through which autos may pass. It is one of two such "drive through" specimens. The old tree suffers no ill effects from its wound, partially caused by fire.

The popular Garberville open-air bus enables
weary drivers to sit back and relax and get a look at
the scenery.

—the silence is broken only by the whisper of wind in the lofty treetops or the occasional song of a bird. It is enough to lift all tension and send a spirit soaring. Visitors tend to speak and tred softly as if loathe to disturb such peace.

On the Bull Creek Flat Road several miles beyond the parking area is **Albee Creek Campground**, and still farther on, the Group Horse Camp and trail.

Upon returning to the Avenue of the Giants at the Dyerville Bridge, you find yourself now moving at a leisurely pace along the west side of the Eel. For ten miles now, the road will wind through more redwood stands and past more dedicated groves until at tiny Pepperwood, you connect with the Avenue's northern access to the freeway and a few more miles of the old scenic highway. Or, you may choose instead to bend westward a hundred yards or so before Pepperwood and take time out to investigate a lumber company's **Demonstration Forest** there. Signs point the way.

One of the more remote and beautiful parts of the
Redwood Empire is the valley of the Mattole River
in Southern Humboldt County.

At this point you are 30 miles south of Eureka and once again on
the freeway, U.S. 101.

Just eight miles beyond Pepperwood—a good place to load up
with home-grown fruits and vegetables at roadside stands—one can
again leave the freeway for a look at a Scotia busy lumber town built
entirely of redwood. Almost everyone here works directly or indirectly
for the Pacific Lumber Company, the world's largest redwood sawmill.

By obtaining a permit at the company office, one may on week-
days follow the white line through the entire operation from millpond
to drying yards. Across the road stands the impressive full-round log
building, once the bank and now a lumber industry museum. It is
interesting that the logs, still feeling like trees, at first continued to
sprout. The bank had to be pruned even after beginning to house the
village's money.

Grizzly Creek Redwoods State Park is the farthest east of the

The other drive-through tree in the Redwood Empire is the Shrine Tree at Myers Flat, just off U.S. Highway 101 in Humboldt County. Burned out ages ago, the tree still lives despite this gaping hole.

Cut off by the freeway are many miles of the old
highway that can be explored at an easy pace, with
little traffic and frequent turn-outs for strolling
among some of the mightiest redwoods.

redwood parks, some 30 miles from the coast in the Van Duzen River Valley. To see it, leave the main highway at Alton, south of Fortuna, and follow winding State Highway 36 eighteen miles along the Van Duzen River, the route used a century ago by cattle ranchers driving their animals to shipping points on the coast—after the Siskyou Indians, once native there, had been relocated farther north on the Hoopa Indian Reservation.

Despite the park's name, no grizzlies are around anymore to disturb your groceries and peace of mind. Vacationers wishing to relax in a primitive area, far from the traveling throngs, seek out this beautifully remote refuge.

Besides the Van Duzen River, Grizzly Creek also waters the park. The preserve features groves of fine old redwoods, a hillside of second growth, a mile of open riverfront campground, and shady picnic sites near park headquarters, which was once the site of a stagecoach stop. Situated beyond the coastal fog belt, the park's climate is mild to warm during the vacation months, and there are excellent facilities for the sojourner. Short trails lead through redwoods, one a self-guiding nature trail, another a somewhat more rugged one, the mile-and-a-half upslope Hikers Trail. Paths go to the river for your sunning and bathing pleasure. During the season, rangers conduct walks and campfire programs and maintain a display interpreting the flora and fauna.

Campers here can expect to see deer, raccoons, skunks—and perhaps a bobcat, if they are lucky. Should the fishermen among them arrive after the so-so trout season, they could well find the fall and winter salmon and steelhead runs to their liking.

Carlotta and Bridgeville, ten miles each way from Headquarters, are adequate supply centers.

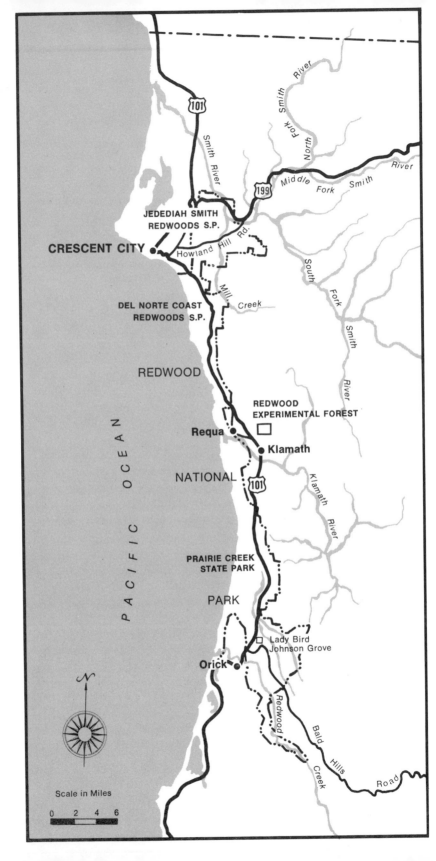

Redwood National Park Country

A dozen miles or so above Fortuna the air begins to change. Now you notice a salty tang in it and become aware of approaching the sea. You pass Fernbridge, then the Lolita turnoff, and all at once see to your left the waters of Humboldt Bay. In a few minutes you come to Fields Landing, where some years ago stood a whaling station, then swing around by the College of the Redwoods and on to **Eureka**, seat of Humboldt County, lumbering and seaport center, the "nation's westernmost city."

The city is noted for its abundance of Victorian homes, well-kept relics of another day, and its Sequoia Park, where ferned trails wind among tall redwoods and their usual associates, past a pond afloat with friendly ducks. Add to this a zoo and Eureka makes for an altogether pleasant stopover for car-weary visitors, especially when combined with a look at Fort Humboldt State Historic Park atop Fort Hill overlooking the bay. Exhibits show earlyday personalities and activity in and near the old bastion. Here served General Ulysses S. Grant in 1853, when it was a federal outpost and he just a captain committed to the protection of pioneers from Indian uprisings.

Redwoods still crowd the eastern borders of both Eureka and Arcata—on the upcoast end of the bay—as they once did the first tiny settlements. Only now they march down into the hillside residential areas and the campus of Humboldt State University. Forests, bay, and sea together constitute vast outdoor classrooms for the serious students of forestry, oceanography, and wildlife and fishery management. Originally named Uniontown, Arcata a century ago was the take-off point for mule trains lugging supplies back to the gold mines of the Trinity. It also served as the locale for many of Bret Harte's stories when he was a reporter on the town's weekly newspaper. Today, in and around Humboldt Bay a huge forest products industry is concentrated. The area is also a center for dairying, commercial fishing, and cattle and sheep raising.

A visitor wishing to picnic in Arcata would like the city's Redwood Park, with its redwood-lined perimeter, nature trails, and adjoin-

*These towering Coast Redwoods near Orick are
367 feet high and are believed to be the tallest
living things on earth.*

ing Community Forest. In fact, everywhere around and farther north, endless diversions await, such as duck and geese hunting in bay and marsh; fishing—deep sea and surf—salmon, steelhead, and trout in the Mad, Eel, and Klamath rivers and their tributaries; deer hunting inland; clamming, and agate and driftwood prospecting on the beaches; photographing and painting of vistas to thrill the soul at hundreds of places along the way.

To see a profusion of colorful and fragrant spring wildflowers, zig off the beaten path to the **Azalea State Reserve** above Arcata on the Mad River. Turn in from U.S. 101 on the North Bank Road, and after parking, pick up one of the self-guiding nature trail leaflets. Then walk beneath spreading masses of Western azalea blossoms. In the late spring and early summer from here on northward, great patches of their pinkish white blossoms brighten the somber green of the forest and cascade over wayside fences. Presently, rhododendrons rising alongside big redwood trunks replace the lower-growing azaleas.

If you happen to be around Humboldt Bay on Annie & Mary Day—the first Sunday in August—you might enjoy a train ride. If so, just north of Arcata, turn inland on U.S. 299 about 4 miles to the tiny village of Blue Lake. The 120-year-old steam Shay locomotive, Spanking Fury, named for the white horse that pulled the first log cars out to the ships, departs from the Blue Lake depot. After boarding full-view open cars, you can relax for a happy hour on an 11-mile rail trip across and along the Mad River and among the redwoods. Not only train buffs, but everyone is sure to love it.

On up the Redwood Highway, the traveler now passes a series of beaches, headlands, and lagoons, some of them bordered in spring and early summer with great dome-shaped masses of yellow bush lupin. Of such is Clam Beach near Little River, north of McKinleyville, at low tide a mecca for moonstone and agate rockhounds.

Three of the four state areas set aside for enjoyment in the next dozen miles are **Little River**, **Trinidad**, and **Dry Lagoon beaches**, all fine for picnicking, clamming, and beachcombing for driftwood, moonstones, and agate. **Patricks Point**, while not in a redwood setting, nevertheless offers an interlocked overhead shelter of pine, fir, hemlock, cypress, and Sitka spruce that together with the verdant patches of tall berry, azalea, and salal bushes, provide natural privacy and shelter for each individual campsite and some protection from the fog that is an almost constant fact of life—night and morning at least. Old Indian trails lead out onto the rockbound point and along the cliffs from which you can hear the sea lions barking on the offshore rocks. One trail pitches steeply down onto the dark sands north of the park, named Agate Beach for the happy hunting grounds of agate, jasper, and black jade.

And who could drive upcoast without turning aside long enough to visit the fishing haven of **Trinidad Bay**, neatly pocketed alongside Trinidad Head, the lighthouse-capped bulge of rock seen for miles from up and down the coast? You'll find available at this popular salmon fishing spot, skiffs, tackle, launching facilities, and party boats. Be sure to ready the camera. Everything along the coast is photogenic.

In this area, you pass a series of picturesque lagoons enclosed by sandbars. Largest of them is Big Lagoon. And then there is the smaller but scenic Stone Lagoon; both lie between Trinidad and Orick. During flood times their brackish waters mingle with the inrushing sea, enabling salmon and steelhead to enter and eventually work their way up the several tributary creeks to spawn. But most fishermen have little trouble any time of the year catching their 3-fish limit of cutthroat trout and small steelhead, always "at home" in these glassy waters. Freshwater Lagoon, just south of Orick, is planted for seasonal trout fishing.

One thing you may notice about the lagoons, aside from their dark reflections and almost mystic aura, is that slowly but surely they are filling with the sediment deposited by their feeder streams. One day, possibly well within your lifetime, they could firm into marshes and from there to broad grassy floodplains, sprinkled with wildflowers and watered by the meandering creeks that created them.

And now the road brings you into little Orick and the southern headquarters of California's 46-mile long **Redwood National Park**, which you are about to enter via the ribbon of Redwood Highway that winds almost the length of it. This is a good place to stop for maps and information.

A right turn off the highway just north of town will lead two miles along the Bald Hills Road to the **Lady Bird Grove**, dedicated in 1968 by Mrs. Lyndon B. Johnson. To reach the **Tall Tree Grove** in the bend on up Redwood Creek, though, you would have to hike in 8½ miles on a trail that takes off along the stream slightly westward of the Bald Hills Road, close to Mill A of the Arcata Redwood Company. Primitive camping is permitted anywhere along Redwood Creek with the exception of ¼ mile either side of the Tall Trees Grove. As the national park is funded and develops its own special trails and facilities, it will offer more and better trails into the back country.

As of now, three of California's 32 state redwood parks, **Prairie Creek, Del Norte Coast,** and **Jedediah Smith,** lie within the 58,000

President and Mrs. Johnson dedicating the Lady Bird Grove. Note also the Nixons on the other side of the plaque.

acre national park created by Congress in 1968 and constitute its main units. Quite naturally these are the centers of activity, for they have long been developed and in them stand some of the most majestic of all coastal giants. Eventually, as the national park Master Plan is converted into action, additional lands obtained from lumber companies will be improved and opened for use.

Without doubt, Prairie Creek is one of the all-time favorite campgrounds in the state. Though a bit on the cool, damp side, yet protected by ridges from the ocean winds, Prairie Creek provides one of the most varied and exciting of all redwood vacations—or day picnics—or just rest stops.

Entering from the south and noticing first the big fenced prairie protecting the only remaining herds of native Roosevelt elk, you begin to see the reason for the love affair. When you turn in, clear the entrance station, and drive or walk the campground, you understand even better. This is a dense forest of lush understory among giant

Largest known coast redwood tree is located in Jedediah Smith Redwood State Park. It measures 20 feet in diameter four feet above the ground. The Stout Tree is named not for its size, but in honor of the family which donated the grove.

redwoods, fir, spruce, and hemlock. Alder and maple line the beautiful creek. Mosses, ferns, and lichen are everywhere, covering downed trees, springing out of every upturned root system, all in the kind of wild and damp profusion one associates with Washington state's Olympic Peninsula rain forest. Each campsite is in itself a verdant scene —somewhat sunny if near the prairie edge; darker, more secluded, dripping with moss if back in the grove near the creek; every bit of it bearing witness to the sopping winters of 100-inch-plus rainfall and the foggy "other season." There are more than 40 miles of excellent trail fanning out from headquarters and through the park's more than 12,000 acres.

Prairie Creek offers a broad beach at the base of high bluffs, solidly populated with redwood forest. For a time in the 1850's, prospectors worked the sands of this remote 8-mile shoreline, hoping to strike it rich, but moving on to more promising fields when the sands did not pay out. This is why this seaside border of Prairie Creek is named, appropriately, Gold Bluffs and Gold Beach. You can hike to it one way by following the 4-mile Miner's Ridge Trail to a beach campground nestled among the dunes or better still, take the wonderfully beautiful although slightly longer James Irvine Trail through a tall fern forest to Fern Canyon, a gash in the bluffs cut by one of the creeks. Nothing less than spectacular, its sheer 50-foot sides drip with sword and five-fingered ferns. For an unforgettable experience, walk the mile or so upcanyon, following the streambed. Where have you seen anything like it!

Three miles south of the park entrance a side road (not for trailers and such) takes off westward past the Davison Dairy and through a logged area to the shoreline, then along the strand for several miles at the foot of the bluffs. From here one can walk Fern Canyon, thus enabling travelers short on time or energy to visit the incomparable canyon of ferns. Elk graze along here, too.

The park entrance area, its checking and ranger stations and visitor center stand at the northern edge of the prairie—or the edge of the forest, depending on how you look at it. There you may obtain maps and information and can inspect the camp and picnic areas bordering a part of the prairie nearby. Or, you may choose to take a unique nature walk, something new and wonderful that has been added to man's viewing and appreciation of the giant redwoods. This time it is especially for the sightless—the Revelation Trail for the Blind at Prairie Creek in the Redwood National Park.

Funded by the Save-the-Redwoods League and constructed by park personnel in 1971, it is a smooth and level half-hour walk for about

Beautiful Little Prairie Creek flows tranquilly through a land of giants.

a quarter of a mile through Prairie Creek's main grove.

Blind visitors first call at park headquarters for interpretive Braille text leaflets. Then, with a hand on the trailside guide rope, they walk the path until a plastic ball on the rope signals a stop.

Each of the numerous stops on the trail provides a redwood forest experience of smell, touch, or hearing that speaks and informs, each in its own way. And so the sightless learns about texture of redwood bark, the depth of duff on the forest floor, the form of a redwoods surface roots, the shape of sword ferns. He listens to the sounds of wildlife, and comes to recognize the various fragrances of trailside plants and flowers. Sighted visitors, seeing the delight of the blind, are brought to the realization of their own good fortune and cherish it more than ever before.

Elk-watching and photographing are of course daytime activities at Prairie Creek, for this is a reserve for these huge animals that once roamed north into Canada and east to Mt. Shasta—and then came close to extinction. Best remember not to try and buddy with them.

Thousands of verdant ferns line the sides of Fern Canyon. This green slice of nature is a mile north of Orick, in upper coastal Humboldt County.

Part of herd of Roosevelt Elk, named in honor of Theodore Roosevelt, are often seen by tourists driving through the meadow of Prairie Creek State Park, Humboldt County.

While not unfriendly, they are nevertheless unpredictable. Look rather than approach, and keep your distance.

There is plenty to see and do in Prairie Creek. From Memorial Day to Labor Day the rangers conduct hikes and nature walks in addition to evening campfires. Excellent surf- and stream-fishing keep the anglers interested and busy landing rainbow and cutthroat trout in the summer, salmon and steelhead in the fall and winter. But swimming or even dunking in the ocean is in the UGH! classification. The surf is icy and dangerous. The dunes, though, are inviting. And if you are a confirmed shutterbug, you'll be challenged by the tall ferns, the masses of azalea and rose-purple rhododendron, the prairie wildflowers, to say nothing of the gigantic forest primeval everywhere around the elk-studded prairie and all the way to the sea.

Leaving park center, you travel for miles past a succession of especially dedicated memorial groves that line both sides of the two-

A quiet day can be enjoyed in the U.S.
Redwood Experimental Forest at Klamath
inspecting the various cuts and learning about
redwood forest regeneration.

lane highway. Almost side by side the trees stand in massive splendor along the soft shoulder with turnouts here and there to suggest pausing awhile for a stroll into the dim and luxurious forest, where, once out of a car, you may simply stand and look and let the peace of ages past flow through you.

Once back at the wheel, and before long, on a wide sweeping curve, you find yourself gazing down onto the great Klamath River, one of the largest on the Pacific Coast, most of it wild and primitive, meandering across its widening flood plain toward the sea from Central Oregon 263 miles away. A mile above the mouth, a high memorial bridge guarded at either end by big golden bears, takes you across with a view in a million thrown in for good measure. Without question, here is California's mecca de lux for fishermen.

On both sides of the river, up and downstream are private campgrounds and fishing resorts enough to delight any vacationer with a yen for haunting stream and sea, birdwatching, or hunting with a camera. Most of the resorts have hookups to accommodate trailers and motor homes; some rent boats and sell tackle, provide ramps and even have fishing guides available. In addition, there are motels, seafood restaurants, a cannery where you can have your catch put-up to take home, a late June Salmon Festival, a jet boat fleet at Requa for day trips far upriver through Indian country and back, a Klamath and Hoopaw Railroad that loops high into the forest to an overlook to remember. You name it and you'll find it in the Klamath River area —at Requa, once an important Yurok Indian village; at little Klamath, relocated since the devastating flood of 1964; at Klamath Glen in Terwer Valley upriver several miles.

In the mild summertime from early July through September, when the big salmon run tapers off, sportsmen from all over the world flock to the Klamath to compete for king and silver salmon. Shorecasters line the rocks and sandspits at the rivermouth and hundreds of boats dot the estuary and offshore waters. Others prefer the upriver riffles and deep pools. Steelhead run from July until the heavy winter rains, after Indian summer has finished daubing the green-clad mountains with yellow and gold. In the spring, summer, and fall, sturgeon and schools of candlefish, followed overhead by flocks of telltale seagulls, head upstream. Cutthroat trout fishing is good all year in the river below the bear bridge.

A dramatic panorama of river and coastline is yours for the driving a mile of winding road from Requa up to the north bluff, topped by a U.S. Radar station. Just below the station gate, a turnoff onto a parking space gives one an opportunity to look safely and perhaps even take the national park trail down the cliffs.

Beyond relocated Klamath a couple of miles on 101 is the federal **Redwood Experimental Forest**, where an area has been set aside for long-range research on redwood forest management and harvesting. In this scientifically controlled forest, various logging methods are tried, all directed toward greater forest vigor and regeneration so that the best management practices can be determined and employed in cutting, reforestation, and conservation of this valuable renewable resource.

A free self-guiding drive leads easily through four square miles of experimental cutover acreages, each with an interpretive sign explaining that particular project, indicating objective, theory, method, difficulties encountered, mistakes made and lessons learned in the process. This side trip is highly informative and relaxing, an off-the-road adventure of real worth.

At Trees of Mystery, a 15-ton, 48-foot Paul Bunyan
towers over fans at the entrance of this private park
several miles north of the Klamath River.

A short distance farther up 101 you all at once come upon a
great deal of activity—the famous Ripley's Believe-it-or-Not **Trees of
Mystery**—a private park and one of the busiest spots on the Redwood
Highway. Dominating the vast parking area are heroic figures of Babe,
the Blue Ox, and Paul Bunyan, several stories high, who speaks
friendly welcoming words to individuals walking toward the big gift
shop, the authentic Indian Museum, and an enclosed park of many
unusual trees and huge wood sculptures, carved with a chainsaw. Although a fee is required to enter the park through a hollow log and
walk the Trail of Tall Tales, a visit offers much of the unique and
traditional. People by the hundreds are attracted. Easter services and
weddings are held at the Cathedral Tree.

From here the Redwood Highway soon passes a small lagoon
wayside stop, and then skirts the sea and an inviting stretch of beach.
At the mouth of Wilson Creek it angles inland through the **Del Norte
Coast Redwoods State Park** unit of the national park.

National Park rangers lead beach walks at Endert's Beach, Crescent City, much to the delight of tidepool enthusiasts.

This beautiful rain forest was the last of the northern redwood parks to be developed. Its well-equipped campground was opened in 1967 in the protected Mill Creek area, two miles by road in from the highway. Look for the directional sign. Here in the alders beside the stream one may camp in mild summer temperatures. Trailerites are welcome, though they will not find hookups in this out-of-the-way setting. The creek is made to order for troutfishing in season, wading, and youngster dunking.

After the prolonged and drenching winter rains (when the park is closed) spring may be a bit early for tent camping at Mill Creek, but if you are there just then and drive down in, you will likely be stunned by the color splashed all over the campground and alongside the road leading to it. The azalea and rhododendron will be at their very best, often lingering into July. A great time for running wild with camera in hand—or just looking. If autumn is your pet season, you'll love the white-barked alders that will have turned yellow and gold in bright contrast to the somber green of the forest.

And this isn't all. Del Norte Coast Redwoods has so much. Luxuriant masses of berry vines, laden with fruit, are waiting to be harvested and made into pies and jams and muffins as the summer progresses. Every manner of groundcover, shrub, and wildflower, fern, moss, and lichen springs into being, seemingly for your special pleasure.

What's more, a variety of trails lead over much of the park's 6000 acres to some incredibly dramatic and enjoyable vistas and adventures. Perhaps the most exciting of all, the Damnation Creek Trail, begins about four miles south of the turn-off road down to the campground, takes the hiker through the finest of old-growth giants to be found along this coast, and drops steeply down 900 feet to a pocket beach and tidepools among shoreline rocks. A photographer's heaven, to be sure. On the way, mighty fluted columns softened by sprays of rhododendron and the vining Oregon grape appear to be mere illusion in the drifting fog. Here the towering forest marches almost to saltwater, stopping at the edge of the rockbound coastline with the sea thundering against it. Wildlife is abundant—deer, elk, and an occasional bear as well as all manner of forest and shore birds.

Descending the road into Crescent City, look for turnoff to the Rellim Redwood Company's demonstration forest, one of the best-maintained in the area. A mile or so in, parking is provided beside a handsome lodge, where on chilly days you'll find a welcome fire in the fireplace. Leaflets for the taking enhance the self-guiding nature trail starting nearby, which leads through an interesting stand of typical north redwood forest. This side trip is worthwhile and informative.

Crescent City, one of redwood country's delightful small towns, was, in the spring of 1964 partially devastated by a tidal wave emanating from the great Alaska earthquake. You wouldn't know it now, though. The ravaged waterfront has become a long park with a picturesque Convention Center, housing lumber industry exhibits. A well-landscaped shopping mall has replaced a destroyed business section. Across the road, overlooking Crescent Bay, stands the imposing Redwood National Park Headquarters, with significant interpretive displays and an information center.

Once a frontier logging and shipping settlement, Crescent City has become a prideful business town, the last outpost before a traveler departs California for Oregon, either by the scenic coast route, U.S. 101, or inland via U.S. 199 to Grants Pass.

Driving the coastal road, one passes Lake Earl, a marshy lagoon, then tiny Smith River, "Easter Lily Capital of the World," Ship

Ashore (which it really is) and Salmon Harbor, all at the mouth of the Smith River, a fascinating area in itself. One can find plenty to see and do around Crescent City and environs. Besides the redwood forests, numerous creeks and the river, the bay and harbor and miles and miles of beach and rugged coastline, there are special treats within the town's city limits to intrigue and entertain a newcomer.

You can walk along Citizen's Dock, built entirely by the town's residents when governmental help failed, and watch the commercial fishing vessels unload their catch. At low tide, pick your way out to the old Battery Point Lighthouse, now an historic museum; maybe relax with some beachcombing in the driftwood that was piled on the sand by last winter's storms south of Sea Wonders Alive and the Undersea Gardens; or drive slowly north of the business district on Pebble Beach Drive for a leisurely look at the jagged sea stacks offshore and the barking sea lions on them and in the surrounding waters. In winter and spring you can find dozens of high spots from which to scan the outer water for passing whales, and in any season there are tidepools without number to investigate—and leave alone for the next fellow's enjoyment. Digging for razor clams on the north beach is popular; and on almost any sunny day, artists can be seen here and there, painting whatever delights their hearts.

The coastal strip offers great reward for the birdwatcher, for here variety knows no limit on birds of varied habitats, especially when it is remembered that this area is on one of the five major bird migration routes, the Pacific Flyway. Everpresent and fun to observe, Jonathan Livingston Seagull and his entire entourage, wheeling and screeching, and making themselves utterly fascinating. You can enjoy them while searching the beaches for agates and bits of bleached driftwood for planters and flower arrangements back home.

Now yearning again for the redwood forest, you may want to head for **Jedediah Smith Redwoods State Park**, 12 miles northeast of town off U.S. 199 on a narrow, winding highway. On the way are vast cutover areas, some still masses of debris, others flower-studded pastures and small home acreages dotted with high—and huge—stumps, now vine covered, some with small trees growing out of them.

The 9000-acre unit, northern gateway of the Redwood National Park, is drained by two streams—Mill Creek and the Smith, flowing across two sides of the park. "Jed Smith" is a camping-picnicking-swimming-sunbathing-nature study-fishing-boating favorite. Within it stand eighteen stately memorial groves. One is the 5000-acre National Tribute Grove of majestic old giants, dedicated as a living memorial to the men and women who served this country in World War II. Far

Autos and mere humans are dwarfed by towering redwood trees, many of them more than 1000-2000 years old and over 300 feet tall, along this old stagecoach road over Howland Hill, east of Crescent City, California, in Jedediah Smith State Park.

enough inland to escape winds sweeping in off the sea, the park provides shady campsites, sunny streamside beaches, and a smooth-flowing river, ideal for water sports deep or shallow, good for summer troutfishing, and one of the state's best for fall and winter salmon and steelhead.

Freeway fugitives, hoping for backroad quiet, should try the exquisitely beautiful **Howland Hill Road** entrance to Jedediah Smith. On it you may see evidences of its having once been an old stagecoach road, corrugated with split redwood logs, when it was the main line from Oregon to Crescent City. Just take off on Elk Valley Road at the southern end of Crescent City, turn toward the Indian Reservation on narrow but well-maintained gravel, and continue to Howland Summit. Then ease down through the heart of the park. Alongside, spires rise impressively and so close that their furrowed trunks can be touched by merely reaching out the car window.

Downcanyon a few miles, a short spur road leads to the awe-inspiring **Stout Memorial Grove** on Mill Creek Flat, where stands the most imposing redwood goliath of them all, the Stout Tree, 340 feet high, 20 feet in diameter.

Walking along the trail through the primeval grove to the river, gazing up the great columns at crowns often lost in fog, visitors invariably sense a pervading serenity and hush. Something about this entire area, dedicated as it is to our nation's defenders, brings out the silence in people, too. Few are surprised to learn that this is reported to be the most heavily timbered acreage in the world.

`During the summertime, rangers relate the history and interpret the enormous variety of flora and fauna—which includes a bear now and then—that populate the park. This, together with excellent camping and picnicking sites and splendid trails through the groves and along the waterways adds up to a wonderful visit at Jedediah Smith.

Sierra Big-Tree Country

Making the grand tour of the Sierra Nevada's 250-mile long range of Big Trees is entirely different from merely following the long Highway 101 through the coastal redwood realm and occasionally branching out from it. You have to work harder in the high mountains. All the seventy-odd groves—some widely spaced, some completely isolated and inaccessible during the winter—may be reached only by winding two-lane roads, much of the way steeply up and down. But they are worth the effort.

North of the Kings River, the stands are scattered, and aside from some magnificent individual sequoias, not as collectively spectacular as toward the south, where they reach the grandeur known round the world.

Moisture they all must have, either as rain or snow or both, wherever that coincides with the best soil drainage. Generally, their elevation preferences extend upward from 7500 feet to somewhat more than 8500 feet and downward from 4500 feet to just over 3000 feet as the latitude warms from north to south on the Sierra's western slope. Reproduction becomes more prolific in the milder southern climate, but essentially the Big Tree groves occupy the same high benchlands that they did when the Sierran glacial rivers carved their natural range into separate and permanent stands.

Even so, these stands are not purely sequoia. As in other forests, they have companion trees—the long-coned sugar pine, the ponderosa, incense cedar and white fir, and in the northern section the Douglas fir, some of them large and impressive. And among them, of course, grow the younger generations.

A sequoia is not really mature until nearly into its second century. By then, its softly conical Christmas tree look and its darkish bark gives way to a reddening trunk, huge, limbless and scarcely tapering for perhaps a hundred feet above the base. In January or February, flowers will appear on the branches, followed in 18 to 20 months by mature egg-size cones, yellow-green to brown and containing 150 to 250 seeds. Many remain on the tree for years or until a chickeree cuts

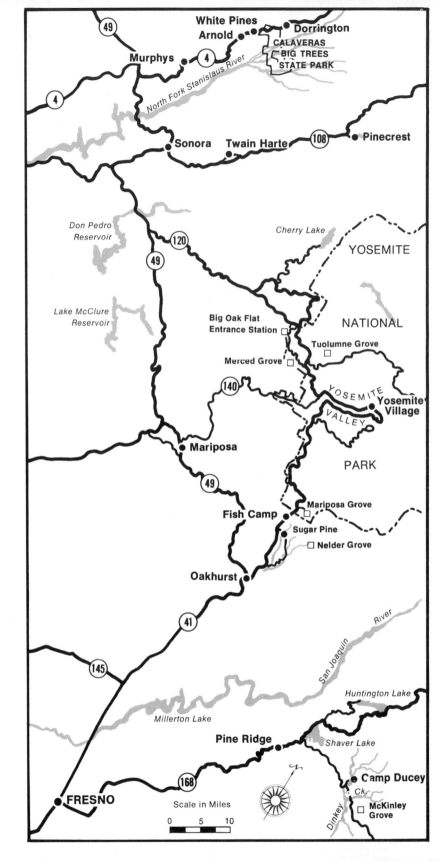

them down. Although millions of paper-thin winged seeds scatter in the winds of the cones' second autumn, a surprisingly small percent are viable and fewer yet reach mineral soil. For one thing, the ground cover of forest litter is too thick. Only where the earth has been disturbed by road maintenance or construction or uprooted trees or the work of some animal, and there is plenty of sunlight and moisture, will you see bushy little sequoias, and then usually by the dozen. Some of them are bound to survive the appetites of hungry wildlife. But nowhere will you find the giants sprouting families around their bases after the manner of the coast redwoods. Since seeds are the only hope of Big Tree reproduction, and despite being borne in great abundance, the density of the forests they produce cannot begin to compare with those found in the mountains along the sea.

As a youthful giant gradually develops a crown that joins others in the sky to form a kind of canopy, the lower limbs are shaded out and fall one by one, doing away with fuel that might cause a ground fire to climb upwards and turn the tree into a torch.

In time, the crown becomes more gnarled. Wind and lightning shatter it. And, too, the flow of moisture and nutrients from the root system to the branches may have been interrupted or severed by fires that have found a break in the bark and destroyed a part of the cambium layer and sapwood. In this case, the loftiest limbs and foliage, deprived of nourishment, die of starvation and are seen as angular and barren arms.

The Big Tree bark is thicker, softer, and much redder than that of the coast redwood and just as immune to extremes of heat and cold, and as good a non-conductor of electricity. In fact, even when a blowtorch is applied, it will not ignite. Only after a portion of the bark is destroyed by a falling limb or tree or burned hotly and long by debris piled against the upslope side of the trunk will a blaze eat into the more vulnerable heartwood. Most old giants have survived so many fires over the centuries that their bases and flanks are deeply scarred; yet most are vigorously healing their wounds.

Unlike the coast redwood foliage, which has distinctive flat sprays with leaves arranged along both sides of the twigs, the Big Tree foliage resembles that of the incense cedar, except that the tiny leaves are awl-shaped and fitted tightly around the stems like sharply pointed scales. Male and female flowers appear on the same stem, and the pollen, released in the spring, drifts in golden clouds, coloring the snow wherever it falls.

The root system is incredibly shallow—6 feet or so with no taproot. Hair-fine feeder roots spread far in all directions, sometimes

General Grant Tree in the Sierra.

200 to 300 feet, twice as far as those of the coast redwood, and they are fully as vulnerable to soil compaction from automobile and foot traffic.

The wood, a salmon pink color, changes to a dark maroon when exposed to the air. It is much lighter in weight than the coast redwood and just as durable although not nearly as strong. The heartwood and bark are so saturated with tannin that they act like an insecticide by repelling insects and resisting decay. As with the coastal giant, the sequoia can lie on or in the ground in almost perfect condition for centuries after the sapwood has disintegrated. In fact, the Big Tree is so heavily endowed with tannic acid that John Muir added water to it and made a usable, deep purple ink.

Nature appears to have prepared both coast redwood and Big Tree for a hoary life span of no telling how many thousands of years. How far this will extend into the future remains to be seen. Doubtless some of the unknown depends upon us.

The Big Trees
of the Central Sierra

At the northern end of the entire range of Sierra Big Tree you would find the small **American River Grove** twenty miles west of Lake Tahoe. Far off the beaten path, tiring to reach, and because it consists of only a half dozen mature trees, it grows in lonely isolation. The most impressive of the northerly stands is the **Calaveras Grove** of Big Trees, some fifty miles downrange. This magnificent grove was the first to be widely known, and is the only state park of Sierran giants.

The Calaveras trees were discovered in the 1850's by a fortyniner named A. T. Dowd. He wasn't the first white man to discover the Big Trees, but being able to tell a story with more pizzaz than anyone of the others, he left an indelible mark on the legends of the Sierra.

Credit for the first recorded sequoia discovery, probably the Merced or Tuolumne grove, undoubtedly goes to Captain Joseph Walker and his expedition, making the first crossing of the Sierra from Salt Lake to Monterey in 1833, and later to John Bidwell and his immigrants who passed through Calaveras Grove in 1841. Following them came a number of others, among whom was one who memorialized his amazement by carving "J. M. Wooster June 1850" on what is now the Hercules Tree in the Calaveras North Grove.

So, though Dowd was a Johnny-come-lately, his astonishment was heard round the world after he chanced upon a grove of trees "taller than the masts of ships and thicker than houses" while in pursuit of a wounded grizzly back in 1852. In great excitement, he reported his discovery to disbelieving miners at Murphy's Camp. Trees that big? Ha! Furthermore, they weren't about to bother following him into the forest for a look.

A few days later the irked but determined hunter tricked them into the grove. Stumbling breathlessly into their midst, he gasped out a story of killing the biggest grizzly he had ever encountered. Now *this* they did have to see. So together they rushed into the forest—into a grove of mammoth trees and a stunning surprise. Dowd's story suddenly came to life and with a bang closed the credibility gap.

Accounts of the incident set off a wave of skepticism in other parts of the country because no one had ever heard of trees as gigantic as these. Nevertheless, the tales of the Sierra's big red giants attracted so many travelers from nearby overland routes that two years afterwards a man was enterprising enough to build a resort hotel in the Calaveras Grove to accommodate all the visitors who came to view what had become "one of the wonders of the world."

Among the guests were several whose fertile promotional minds dreamed up ways of exhibiting the giants just to prove their existence to the unbelievers. One man had the bark peeled off a huge sequoia 60 feet up the trunk, then cut into sections. These were sent by clipper ship around Cape Horn to New York. But when workmen started assembling the sections in a building on Broadway, they found that the ceiling of the first floor wasn't high enough. They had to cut holes in the two floors above before they could set the ersatz tree upright and people could come to gape at it—after paying a suitable admission fee.

Soon thereafter, in 1854, an Englishman hired workmen to erect scaffolding around the mightiest sequoia in the grove up as high as 116 feet—the height of a ten-story office building or an oil derrick —so they could remove its bark, which proved to be 18 inches thick at the base. This massively beautiful tree, known as the Mother of the Forest, 365 feet tall, over 20 feet in diameter, he shipped to Sydenham, England, and set it up on the only building in the country big enough to hold such a whopper—the Crystal Palace. People came from everywhere to see it and stare in amazement.

Back in the Calaveras Grove, the ghostly giant, stripped of its protective fireproof bark, stood bare for years, fighting for life. Finally,

This 1872 photograph of 126 men and women aboard a Big Tree stump that was used first as a dance floor, then later, when roofed-over, as a drug store, inn and at last as a newspaper office.

after one of the great fires that swept the forest, it gave up entirely. What was once a majestic tree is today only a blackened snag.

Another enormous sequoia fell victim to five men who laid to with axes to see if they could chop it down. For 23 days they labored with every cutting tool then known. Only after two smaller trees were felled against the giant did it finally thunder earthward. The stump surface, 24 feet in diameter at 8 feet above the ground and showing rings that dated back 2 centuries before the Holy Roman Empire, was smoothed, covered with a pavillion, and used as a dance floor that could accommodate 16 couples at the same time. The huge trunk, not to be wasted, was converted into a bowling alley.

Calaveras Grove of Big Trees State Park contains two groves of sequoias: the well developed North Grove, set aside in 1931; and the larger South Grove, bordering both sides of Big Trees Creek for more than three miles, set aside in 1954 and opened to the public in 1969.

Thanks to the Save-the-Redwoods League and the Calaveras Grove Association, their protection from further atrocities was guaranteed.

The **North Grove**, long a prime favorite of vacationers, is a busy spot in every season. Of a summer, the park naturalists conduct camp-fire programs and lead hikes out among the many dozens of enormous sequoias that are photogenic at any time of year. Certainly Calaveras is a natural playground, especially in the wintertime, when carefree snow bunnies and sled and toboggan enthusiasts can romp on the slopes without concern, for here no ski trails or lifts are provided. North Campground, therefore, is open year-round although necessarily subject to winter weather restrictions, and a joy depending upon whether or not one has a well insulated trailer or camper for the cold months. This goes for organized groups, too, of up to 150 members and for both picnicking and camping. Winter reservations, though, must be made ahead of time.

A number and variety of scenic trails traverse the park's 5500 acres of mountains, grassy meadows, river, canyon, and stands of giant sequoias. Most popular of them all is the self-guiding nature loop walk through the North Grove. It takes off near the campfire circle, where you may pick up a leaflet that will lead you past the largest of the Big Trees, including the Big Stump and the champ—the Empire State, 19 feet in diameter at breast height; in spring, past the snowy display of dogwood that often remains through early summer. Another path, the Lava Bluffs Trail, affords wide views of a landscape created by past volcanic activity. From it, a hiker may also look down into the deep canyon of the Stanislaus River's North Fork.

Larger and more beautiful than the Calaveras North Grove is the park's fire-scarred **South Grove**, ten miles distant from Headquarters by twisting but paved road. There stands the king of the sequoias, the Louis Agassiz Tree, not as tall as many but 22 feet in diameter. And there lies a fallen sequoia, its burned out interior a black cave 30 feet long and 10 feet high. The road ends at Beaver Creek nearly a mile from the canyon and its sequoia-covered slopes. But the utter peace of such a magnificent sanctuary as this makes the short walk pure pleasure. The red-trunked trees are ancient and massive, their stately neighbors—the tall sugar pine, the ponderosa, white fir, incense cedar, oak, and maple—fitting companions for mammoths of the plant world. Seen among them and in the outlying areas along river and ridges are California mule deer and Columbian black-tailed deer, bear, raccoon, porcupine, and squirrels scampering about.

Calaveras Big Trees State Park camp areas and its day-use picnic grounds near Headquarters and on the North Fork offer adequate

*The giants of Calaveras-Big Tree State Park dwarf
all beings moving around their bases. These are of
the North Grove.*

facilities. Swimming in the river pools and sunbathing on the flat water-polished ledges is fun; and fishing for rainbow trout usually proves to be good.

Situated between 4500 and 5500 foot elevations, the band of the Sierra's vigorous forests, the park may be reached from Stockton via several routes to Angels Camp in the Mother Lode, thence 24 miles up on the Ebbetts Pass Highway to Arnolds, the nearest supply center.

Yosemite National Park

Within Yosemite National Park lie three Big Tree groves. The northernmost, the **Tuolumne**, can be found on the old Big Flat Road, now a 17-mile one-way loop beginning at Crane Flat. In 1878 the road was routed through the grove's most noteworthy exhibit, a dead, burned-out stump, tunneled to permit passage of stages to and from the park. (It is too small for today's trailers and motor homes, by the way.) The **Merced Grove**, a fairly large area of scattered sequoias is reached only by a steep road taking off from State Route 120 to Crane Flat and down into a mountain hollow.

By far the most magnificent of the three groves—in fact of all groves north of the Kings River—is the world famous **Mariposa Grove** near the park's south entrance, where a visitor may walk among some of the largest and oldest trees on earth. No longer is driving in there permitted. Long ago the impact of humanity was discovered, and before the giants could succumb to the combination of wheels and feet, the wheels were outlawed so that over a half million travelers a year might at least continue to visit on foot. A parking area is provided at the edge of the grove from which free shuttlebuses offer 5 mile rides into the Big Trees that include interpretive talks by rangers en route.

Quite possibly the **Wawona Tree**, Mariposa Grove's most photographed giant, might still be standing today had it not been driven through so continuously for so many decades. But for years, almost any weekend and vacation day pedestrians tramped around its perimeter, and cars by the hundreds passed through, each pausing long enough for a family snapshot before giving way to the next in line.

Back in 1881 two men with axes and saws were paid $75 to enlarge a burn in the base. What they did was chop a tunnel 8 feet wide, 26 feet long and 10 feet high so to accommodate the passage of horse-drawn stagecoaches, at that time bringing visitors into Yosemite Valley from Merced and Mariposa. Ever since, millions of tourists have passed through the base of that 234-foot tall 26-foot wide mammoth sequoia, slowing down its growth rate and doing no telling how much damage to its general health. That is, they did until 1969, when on one morning in May of that year, rangers clearing snow found the giant stretched out in the drifts. It had toppled under the weight of a record snowfall and admiration lovingly bestowed by almost a century of sightseers from all over the world.

This makes one wonder how long the other giants of Mariposa Grove will be able to withstand the awe and affection of their Public.

One, the **Fallen Monarch**, wasn't as enduring as the Wawona Tree. Its time came prior to the memory of anyone living. You can see it near the entrance to the grove—prone on the forest floor but still well preserved. A man standing beside it looks small indeed. So also did the stagecoaches, loaded with passengers and pulled by six horses atop its great trunk, when they had their picture taken there.

But there are 200 huge old sequoias of ten feet and more in diameter and countless smaller ones still standing to delight the visitor. Perhaps a thousand years before Christ, two giants of about the same height and size leaned companionably against each other until they became one, their tissues united, the roots of each serving both. We know them as the **Faithful Couple**. The **Clothespin Tree** seems to be standing on two legs. Hot fires in the base have shaped the trunk like an old-fashioned clothspin, which presents an odd sight. Near the Museum are the **Four Guardsmen**, tall, erect, of uniform size, lined up in military formation, fitting sentinels for the cabin they look down upon.

It is hard to believe that once all of these were tiny seedlings. Looking at the young sequoias, so bushy and perfectly shaped, you wonder how they can possibly grow to be old and massive and gnarled like the others. Take for instance the **Grizzly Giant**—most dramatic of Mariposa Grove's legion of giants; over 200 feet high, 37.4 feet in base diameter, 100 feet around and still growing faster than many of the trees.

That one is really spectacular. Its great twisted limbs appear to be trying to hold up the sky. On stormy nights, when thunder is shaking the earth, they can be seen against the brilliance of the light-ning flashes in defiance of the elements. Just how the Grizzly stands is one of the forest mysteries. It has a definite lean; four-fifths of its bark and sapwood at the base has been destroyed by fire and the great

Many of the Big Trees have enormous burn-hollows in their bases such as this California Tree —its root system now being carefully protected from visitor trampling.

battered crown struck repeatedly by bolts of lightning—six times in one storm. Any tree not destined to live on through the ages and continue growing as well, would have surrendered long ago to forces as horrendous as these. Just how many centuries this monster has so far endured cannot be determined until its time finally comes and the rings can then be counted, but foresters estimate that the Grizzly Giant has already been growing for perhaps 3500 years.

Near the Grizzly Giant stands the 232-foot **California Tree**, tunneled and stagecoached through in 1895, but now for walking visitation only. Across the road from the Fallen Monarch, the **Corridor Tree**, badly fire-hollowed, remains upright although nourished by only six slender contacts with the ground. The **Telescope Tree**, still living and growing even with its heartwood completely burned out for at least a century, offers the visitor a blackened tube through which to gaze up at a round patch of sky. And no better example is there than the fallen **Massachusetts Tree**, 280 feet long, 28 feet in diameter, to show at once the brittleness of the Sierra sequoia and its system of preservation even after death. This giant toppled in a 1927 storm after becoming weakened by the road that passed nearby. In the crash of its fall, the big tree broke into a number of fragments both crosswise and lengthwise; yet notice how the tree's dark tannin fluids have flowed over the jagged fractures, sealing out insects and fungi and preserving the wood of trunk and limb.

Another giant, appropriately named the **Stable Tree**, was used for that purpose when still standing. Its burned-out interior had once made a perfect shelter for a number of horses. In 1934 it fell victim to windthrow during a violent storm

There are innumerable big sequoias in the Mariposa Grove, awesome in size and age, all with cinnamon-red trunks that would require two dozen or so people, hands clasped, to encircle. Most of their lower limbs branch out more than a hundred feet above ground and are as big through as ordinary forest conifers.

Also of great interest to visitors are the exhibits both in and around the **Mariposa Grove Museum**, a rustic log cabin erected on the site of an historic shelter built in 1857 by a Massachusetts furniture maker who had earlier come to Mariposa, then Wawona, and taken up land there in the meadow to recover from tuberculosis. This pioneer, named Galen Clark, was destined to play an important role in the development of Yosemite.

At first, Clark pitched his tent in the grasses, then for a time tramped the country, hunting and fishing, acquainting himself with the area and making friends with the Indians. But having heard of incredi-

School kids line up before one of
the big ones of the McKinley Grove
to show just how gigantic
its trunk is.

bly huge red-trunked trees already discovered in 1849 by a Major
Burney of Mariposa, he was anxious to find them. And so he kept
looking, until he at last walked into the grove he had heard so much
about a few miles north of his camp. Straightway, he named it for the
county in which it stood—Mariposa.

Thereafter, Clark's Station, as Galen's camp was called, became
the objective of an increasing number of travelers, who came to enjoy
his cooking and be guided through the grove of giants and into Yosemite Valley. John Muir, John and Jessie Fremont, Ralph Waldo Emer-
son, and many other noted folk were among his guests.

The year 1864 turned out to be an important one for Mariposa
Grove and Yosemite. President Abraham Lincoln signed a bill granting
both to the State of California. Congress then directed the Governor to
form a Board of Commissioners to administer the area, and Galen
Clark was invited to serve. Two years later, he was further honored by
being designated Guardian of the Grant, and he acted in this capacity

*Loggers in the early days weren't about to tackle a
giant sequoia's base with an axe. But to make a try
25-30 feet above the root swell where the trunk
slimmed a bit.*

for many years, devoting himself to publicizing Yosemite to the world.
Always on hand to welcome visitors and help them enjoy the trees and
valley and wildlife during their stay, Galen Clark became a familiar and
colorful figure. Not only did he recover his health in the doing, but far
into old age he regaled his guests with stories around the campfire, led
hikes—some of them rugged—and pointed out the wonders of geology
and Nature. Finally he retired in 1896, six years after Yosemite was
created a national park.

On March 24, 1910 Galen Clark passed away and was buried in
the Pioneer Cemetary, Yosemite Valley, at a site he, himself, had
selected and prepared. For 54 years he had been as much a part of
Yosemite country as the Big Trees and the great valley of granite walls.

Two lesser known Big Tree groves lie south of Yosemite's southern gateway between Yosemite and Kings Canyon national parks.

If it's a cutover area you'd like to see, perhaps **Nelder Grove** in
the Sierra National Forest is the one. It has the typical high stumps of

earlyday logging, but to get around requires some doing in places because of a resurgence of growth following the cutting. There is a small campground and The Shadow of the Giants self-guiding nature trail alongside the dirt road winding in from Sugar Pine on State Highway 41. In the area are many patches of young sequoias, each of them about the same age and replacing the big ones that were cut at different times before the turn of the century between 1888 and 1892, and the pines and firs that were harvested in the first three decades of the 1900's. Because of their enormous size, the largest of the sequoias were left untouched.

Management plans call for protection and growth of these giants and the encouragement of the young ones. Dense stands of the younger timber will be thinned by low intensity burns; the older white woods, which compete so vigorously with the sequoias, will be sold and logged out. Recreation and interpretive facilities are to be added. Musts here are the Bull Buck Tree and Old Forester Tree near the campground and in the northwestern section of the grove, Grandad and the Grandkids; not far away the Graveyard of the Giants—each name quite descriptive of what you can expect to find.

The other stand, the **McKinley Grove**, reached from near Shaver Lake on State Highway 168, is really remote. It has something going for it through—if you don't mind plowing through trail-less underbrush and working your way along the creek and upslope to some splendid sequoias. Don't look forward to campgrounds or services here, but you will find a small picnic area and a scenic vista point just north of the grove, and a parking space and restrooms at the entrance. For the young and hardy—the hardy, anyway—McKinley Grove could provide rewarding adventure.

Sequoia and King's Canyon National Parks

Sequoia National Park not only carries the name of the tree itself but is invariably the Promised Land to anyone seeking Big Trees for the first time. To many, "Sequoia" means the spectacular photographs and paintings and poems—the subject and inspiration of everything that represents the vast majestic, the ancient, the *most* of all living things. Even to Californians, long accustomed to superlatives and a superabundance of natural wonders, Sequoia and Kings Canyon national parks are where you go to see the sequoias, for it is here on the Sierra's western slope south of the Kings River that the big red giants have reached the zenith of their development. It is here that groves become forests, closely spaced. And these are the greatest of the Big Tree forests. In them is the ultimate of all plant life.

And so for the traveler it is 36 miles up the narrow State Highway 198 from Visalia to the Ash Mountain Park Headquarters and Hospital Rock; then 16 miles—from Ash Mountain to Giant Forest—of upsadaisy switchbacks and lariats through cooling air and several life zones; past the Four Guardsmen flanking the road; on still higher into the park's best-known attraction, Giant Forest, high on a benchland between the canyons of the Marble and Middle forks of the Kaweah River.

You are now on the **General's Highway** and everywhere around are enormous sequoias, towering massively over the little rustic buildings of **Giant Forest Village**, the park's picturesque supply center. Quite naturally everyone gets out of the car and gawks at the enormous Sentinel tree towering mightily over the toy village and its midget humans. Here is a setting like no other. It takes a spot of time and thought to absorb.

Then, what next?

For starters, you may wish to start at the Lodgepole Visitor Center to see exhibits and get your bearings. By studying the exhibits you can learn something of the geology and history and a bit about the Big Tree forest, its plants and wildlife. In leaving, pick up a National Park Trail Map to guide leisurely strolls of your own choosing and at

Kings River

CONVERSE BASIN

INDIAN BASIN

Hume Lake

180

Evans Grove

Cedar Grove

General Grant Grove

KINGS CANYON

BIG STUMP BASIN

WHITAKER'S FOREST

NATIONAL

Redwood Mountain

PARK

Generals

River

Lost Grove

Dorst Campground

Muir Grove

Hwy

198

SEQUOIA

Giant Forest

BEARPAW MEADOW

CRESCENT MEADOW

Kaweah River

Redwood Meadow Grove

NATIONAL

Middle Fork

North Fork

Kaweah

East Fork

Kaweah

Kaweah

Three Rivers

Skinner Grove

Atwell Mill Campground

Silver City

Mineral King

Kaweah Lake

198

South Fork

Kaweah

River

PARK

Clough Cave

Clough Cave Ranger Station

Garfield Grove

N

Scale in Miles

0   5   10

your own pace. Since it's your first day at 6400 feet, short walks on the level are indicated after a casual exploration of the tiny village.

Then perhaps comes a short drive to **Crescent Meadow**, where you can park and set out on foot around this beautiful grassy clearing to inspect the famous Tharp's Log.

On the way, though, there is much to see on all sides, such as the stately Parker Group named for a U.S. Cavalry officer, the unusual Triple Tree (three growing from a single base), several burned-out sequoias and two huge fallen giants. One, the Auto Log, is for driving up onto for picture taking; another, the Tunnel Log is for driving through and under. It fell across the road several decades ago but a cut was made on the underside so vehicles less than 8 feet high may pass beneath. The others must use a bypath.

Then comes the inevitable query, "Where is the General Sherman, the world's largest living thing?" This, the whole world wants to see.

It is located half way between the Giant Forest Village and the Lodgepole Visitor Center. Just follow the Generals Highway 2 miles from the village to the **General Sherman** parking area.

And suddenly, there it is—the big one! The one on all the calendars and in all the magazines and textbooks—your fourth grade readers; wide as a city street, a hundred feet higher than Niagara Falls, containing enough lumber to build a small town; still growing and producing seeds although bearing black scars of many fires, one that occurred after the fall of the Holy Roman Empire and before the discovery of America. The General is today in excellent health, and no telling how much longer it will stand. Gazing up at it, you read in your trail guide that the first limb, so high above, is longer than most forest trees east of the Mississippi are tall—140 feet. So now just try and take a picture of all that. If this isn't a challenge to your photographic know-how, nothing is.

From the General Sherman by all means follow the **Congress Trail** through its entire easy 2-mile loop. Rising alongside it are giants almost as large as the General Sherman—the Lincoln, President, and McKinley trees, all stately and splendidly red-trunked. There is the Leaning Tree, slowly being undercut by a stream, but striving valiantly to right itself by curving away from the direction it would fall.

Here and there you notice blackened giants, seared by ancient fires in debris that had accumulated against their boles and had burned so long and hotly that they finally ate through bark a foot or two thick,

Giant Forest Village provides a cafe, gift shop,
grocery for visitors and a natural stopping
place for gazing upward in open-mouthed wonder.

and consumed much or all of the heartwood. The Telescope Tree is such. Ring counts on downed sequoias show when these fires occurred and that the last serious conflagration was about 200 years ago. Notice also the fire scars that are gradually being covered with spreading cambium layer and bark. The ability of a sequoia to seal over its wounds in this manner clearly demonstrates its tremendous capacity for self-renewal.

Seeming to preside over Circle Meadow is the **Senate Group** and the nearby **House Group**, two stands of magnificent sequoias, collectively the grandest of all groups in the Sierra. More than any, they represent the most nearly perfect, the most symetrically formed giants in the Sierra.

Near the **Founders Group**, dedicated to those who were responsible for the saving of this second national park in 1890, you will find a fallen giant. This one is interesting because its upturned root

*The General Sherman—largest and one of the oldest
living things—and still growing older and larger.*

Hale Tharp

HALE THARP, A PIONEER STOCK-man and homesteader in the Three Rivers area, a good and friendly man, was always kind to the Potwisha Indians who were his neighbors. He was pleased when they came to look at him. After all, they were curious about him, for he was the first white man they had ever seen. To show Chief Chappo and his Indians that he liked them, Tharp shot deer for their food supply. Because they didn't have any firearms of their own, they were understand-ably delighted.

In return, they told Tharp about great red-trunked trees that grew in the mountains above and offered to lead him to them. Wondering if such giants as those described really could exist, Tharp accepted their offer. Early one summer, when in the company of several Indians he set out up the Middle Fork of the Ka-weah River below the great bulge of Moro Rock.

Sure enough, there stood the giants—a whole forest of the mightiest trees the world would ever see. In order to record the momentous occasion, Tharp carv-ed his name H. D. Tharp and the date, 1858, in a huge sequoia log hollowed by fire. Later he built an entryway with door at the butt end, fashioned a window, a rock fireplace, bunk, table and bench.

For thirty summers after that, Hale Tharp pastured his stock in the high meadows of this forest, each time living in the big burned-out log. His "home" was spacious, snug, and comfortable; one room 56 feet long, tapering from 24 feet high at the entrance to 4 feet at the other end. The tree was estimated to have stood 311 feet tall when in its full glory.

system shows so well how little there is that holds these mammoth trees upright.

If you've never been inside a tree, here's your opportunity. By climbing a short ladder you can enter the Room Tree through a burn, go down into the room, and exit through a blackened opening in the other side.

In this small Big Tree community is all manner of forest inhabit-ants from the young bushy sequoias to the aged veterans of countless centuries that show the full range of natural disasters they have en-dured in their long lifetimes. Seen with them are their associates —especially the white fir and stately sugar pine, their trunks gilded with staghorn lichen. All the while the forest rings with the raucous squawk of Steller's jays as they bicker with the Douglas squirrels—or

In 1875 John Muir visited Tharp and called his home "a noble den". Gazing up at the massive sequoias all around, he named the place The Giant Forest, which it has remained to become the heart of Sequoia National Park.

Tharp's log house is still there. You can find it easily at Crescent Meadow, an easy short walk from where you park your car.

chickerees—which, by the way, are experts at gnawing off sequoia cones and conking visitors on the head with them. And who could fail to see the golden mantled ground squirrels scampering about, eyes bright, tails flirting this way and that as they figure the best ways to con admiring humans.

In the flower-studded meadows California mule deer browse peacefully undistrubed by the proximity of visitors, and occasionally a bear will make his presence known, clawing the bark of a downed tree in search of grubs or simply rolling in the grasses or carpet of lupine.

The **Congress Trail** walk can take you an hour or a day, but it is pleasant, easy, and awe-inspiring to visit in the early morning, when the great red trunks appear to glow and shutterbugs run miles of color film through their cameras.

Sometimes it's easier to cut through a thing than to try and remove it. Anyway, this is something unique in an archway. On the road to Moro Rock.

Wherever a visitor decides to linger—in the Lodgepole or Dorst campground (no electrical or sewer hookups) or in the housekeeping cabins at the Lodge—big trees, whether they be sequoias or pines, firs or cedars, will be just outside. And almost anywhere you look, where soil has been turned, youngster sequoias, green and conical reach for the sun.

In climbing Moro Rock for a look at the jagged skyline of the Great Western Divide or watching the fadeout of day from either Beetle or Sunset Rock, the visitor becomes aware of still more giants not far away. And should one elect to hike or ride one of the available saddle horses into the back country—to Alta Peak, Bear Paw Meadow, Redwood Meadow, the John Muir Trail or distant Mt. Whitney—he will move for some time through Big Tree forests before emerging onto solid granite and a wide view of the Sierra's lofty spine.

All seasons in this band of national parks and forests claim their devoted fans. Winter sports or just sightseeing or plain flopping around in snow among the big red giants attracts the young and hardy; spring draws those who hanker to watch life blossom clean and new—the azaleas, the dogwood, the snowplant, and the everchanging myriads of small flowers rising in the meadows. Summer, signaling vigor and laziness at the same time, attracts hordes of families with youngsters happily sprung from school and bursting with the spirit of go and do. Fall, offering tranquillity after the rush and the aura of Nature preparing for a long rest, draws the retireds, the older generations, to enjoy a time of relaxation and contemplation. Sounds are sharp and colors brightly warm against the ever-green.

Leaving Giant Forest Village and winding along the all-weather General's Highway past Lodgepole and Dorst campgrounds, you bisect the beautiful Lost Grove and head for **Grant Grove**, preserved in 1890 as General Grant National Park. In 1940 it and the extensive Redwood Mountain Grove were included in the new Kings Canyon National Park.

Before going on into the village, though, you may feel energetic enough to hike into a really splendid stand of sequoias, the **Muir Grove**. Rangers lead guided hikes into this small isolated grove from the Dorst Campground, a five-hour sack lunch excursion well worth the time. If your time is limited, you can also take off on your own. The trail is pleasant, mostly easy, and only five miles round-trip—and what a primitive stand of giants you can see! Hundreds of big ones cover 300 acres, singly and in clusters enough to delight the most reluctant of believers.

Anyway, 30 miles from Giant Forest Village you come to **Grant Grove Village** at the 6500-foot level beside a meadow and near Grant Grove, largest grove of sequoias in Kings Canyon National Park. It is of course the hub of the park with the usual tourist facilities: Park Headquarters and Visitor Center exhibiting splendid displays, the Lodge, coffee and gift shops, post office, service station and store. Ranger naturalists conduct walks and, during the summer, evening campfire programs.

Close beside the road stands the **General Grant Tree**, named to honor the Civil War hero and later President of the United States. Probably the world's second largest tree, it stands 267 feet tall, over 40 feet across at the base, and several thousand years old. Since 1926 the General has been recognized as The Nation's Christmas Tree, and by decree of Congress in 1956 was declared a national shrine dedicated "to the memory of the men and women of the Armed Forces who fought and died to keep this nation free." Every December holiday season, religious and patriotic services are broadcast from the snow at its base.

Sequoia National Park is kept open during the winter.

There are many very large and unusual sequoias in **General Grant Grove** as well as fine specimens of sugar pine, white fir, yellow pine, cedar and birch. Second largest is the towering General Lee Tree. Beside it lies the Fallen Monarch, a burned-out log, down long over a century, used as a stable by cavalrymen who patrolled the park in the 1890's. Everyone admires the George Washington Tree and the stately California Tree, one of the tallest of sequoias and located just right for photographing.

Why didn't lumbermen cut these giants when each contained enough lumber for thirty or forty buildings? Giant Forest would probably have been obliterated had not the forests been acquired by conservationists. In 1890, the National Geographic Society raised $100,000 and together with the National Park Service bought some 250 square miles of Big Tree forest, including these groves, before the sawmills could move in. Since then more than 350 square miles have been added.

Not fortunate enough to have been so lovingly preserved were many forests south of the Kings River Canyon, among which was the four-mile long **Converse Basin** north of Grant Grove. Here loggers committed one of the most revolting butcheries of all time.

In 1885 two San Francisco lumbermen gained title to considerable forest land adjacent to and including the basin. They built their first sawmill near the present-day northern boundary of Kings Canyon National Park below Grant Grove, stripped the area known as Millwood of its Big Trees, and in 1890 began floating the roughcut lumber down to Sanger in the San Joaquin Valley in a 54-mile V-shaped flume, itself an engineering sensation.

By 1897 the clearcut and milling operation had slopped over into the Converse Basin and altogether devastated what was probably the greatest of all primeval forests—a valley of giants, some of which undoubtedly exceeded even the vast bulk of the General Sherman. For years on end, then, down crashed the oldest and mightiest trees that ever stood on earth, one after another, over 8000 acres of them. Destruction was almost total. General Grant Grove is the principal survivor of that vanished splendor. Not that such an extensive operation proved to be profitable. Anything but. As if in defiance, the 1000-ton sequoias shattered like glass when they crashed, and the chunks were so monstrous that only dynamite could reduce them to manageable 20-foot logs that could be handled with axe and 22-foot crosscut saws, hoists and Dolbeer donkey steam engines. Such feats of strength and primitive engineering were surely phenomenal, but so also was the waste, especially in view of the fact that the Big Tree wood was too soft and brittle for structural building.

Nevertheless, aided by three giant bandsaws, one the world's largest, the valley of greatness died, brutally and uselessly, and was abandoned—a graveyard of mammoth stumps, eventually to be absorbed in Sequoia National Forest.

Today, isolated and silent, it stands as a monument to the magnitude of man's greed and folly, his utter disregard of Nature's wonders. Left standing at the northern end of the basin was the **Boole Tree**, named for the man who managed the obliteration of the Converse Basin. No one knows why they left this tree, one of the largest of all. Perhaps its 269-foot height and 35-foot breadth was too much to handle; perhaps someone balked at leveling anything so grand. At any rate, one of the really big ones, it stands today, towering testimony to what might have been had certain men sought elsewhere for riches.

Better check at Headquarters before you seriously contemplate tackling the steep jeep road down in there. It's no freeway.

Another jeep road winds its way into the **Chicago Stump** area just south of the Converse Basin. In there you could drive a couple of miles through a heavily logged and repeatedly burned section, but one where many young sequoia seedlings are rising hopefully out of the blackened ruins. You wouldn't be able to miss the Chicago Stump. It is the pitiful charcoal remains of a giant once known as the General Noble Tree and thought then to have been the monarch of all living things; one so huge and impressive that in 1892 loggers made their cut 50 feet above the ground, hollowed out the stump, and split it into sections, which they then shipped to the Chicago World's Exposition. There, workmen reassembled the pieces for public amazement. Ironically, the viewers were not amazed. They simply rejected the exhibit as a fake!

For a close look at another axed area, leave your car at the **Big Stump** parking and picnic area, pick up a descriptive leaflet from the dispenser box and take the mile-long self-guiding nature trail. Walking this trail you will see a wide variety of logging leftovers along the way—even a sawdust pile and what remains of a felled giant cut into shakes and shingles. You will also find the original corduroy road, the old mill site, and a trench into which a sequoia was once felled to cushion the crash and thus try to save it from fracturing to pieces. But three unique Big Tree remains may interest you even more. One is the Burnt Monarch, estimated to be about 2500 years old and probably the largest sequoia before it was destroyed by fire a century or two ago. Now, only a blackened snag, it is nevertheless imposing, being 97 feet in circumference and perhaps 50 or 60 feet high.

*This was the stump of the General Noble Tree as it
was being cut into sections for shipment
—and before the fires that left it a blackened
monument to man's stupidity.*

The Mark Twain Tree measures 24 feet across after loss of bark
and sapwood, and was by ring count, just under 1500 years old. Two
choppers sweated 13 days felling that giant in 1891—all so that New
York's American Museum of Natural History could exhibit a section of
Big Tree.

The Sawed Tree is in a class all by itself. Apparently its undercut had been made and the tree was being prepared for felling when
for some reason the operation was halted. Yet the giant stands, healthy
and vigorous, the wound gradually healing itself while the uncut side of
the tree supplies it sufficiently with nutrients.

Still other devastated groves are in the **Indian Basin** on the
main highway between the intersections with Hume Lake Road and
the loop to Converse Mountain. It's a walk-through area of big stumps,
small sequoias and thriving second growth. Hume Lake, too, once
extensively logged between 1910 and 1917 is now a takeoff point for a

None of the 23 people atop the Mark Twain stump could possibly feel crowded.

dozen or more groves of sequoias south and east of there, either by trail or jeep road. You may want to try the new road from Hume Lake to Evans Grove, easily the best of all groves of this area. The several hundred Big Trees in there are stately and seem to invite a leisurely walk amongst them.

Favorite gateway to the Sierra's high country is **Cedar Grove**, 30 miles from Grant Grove over State Highway 180 and down into the spectacular canyon of the Kings River's South Fork. Here you can leave your car and backpack or obtain saddle horses for lengthy treks over some of the 900 miles of wilderness trail—or just enjoy a few hours exploring the easy walks around Cedar Grove, visiting the Park Service Information Center and the village, perhaps staying overnight at one of the summer season's cabins, where accommodations are strictly first-come-first-served.

On the General's Highway a few miles south of Grant Grove Village, you will come to an open vista point—**Redwood Mountain Overlook**. By all means hold up here a minute to scan the panorama.

From this spot you can view a wide expanse of densely forested mountain and canyon, known as Redwood Mountain Grove, largest stand in Sequoia National Forest, and some say the most magnificent of the Big Tree groves. It could well be a kind of orientation stop if you were planning to drop 1.7 miles down into that canyon from the General's Highway (5 miles south of Grant Grove Village) for a hike.

Along the canyon floor or the slopes above, you would walk through very heavy stands that are almost purely Big Tree and contain the Hart Tree, one of the largest of sequoias. Furthermore, here you would find peace and quiet and escape from vacationing crowds.

In the **Sugar Bowl**, 2½ miles from the nearest traveled road, grows the purest stand of all—and probably all yours, too, because of its isolation. Everywhere around are the huge red trunks of towering giants, seeming to cluster together in some kind of sequoia-only conclave. This 8-mile, full-day loop, should you choose to hike it, is one you will never forget. But if you can't stoke up that much time or energy, there are shorter walks to Sugar Bowl, about five miles, and to Barton Flats, just half that distance. And you can take these either on your own or in guided hikes from Grant Grove Village.

Of interest to note at this point is the 320-acre section of Redwood Mountain Grove known as **Whitaker's Forest**. Deeded in 1910 to the University of California by an eccentric recluse who bought the tract and pioneered there in the solitude of the early 1900's, it has been used for forestry experimentation and instruction, as Whitaker had requested.

The concept of scientific forest management has been on the rise for several decades in forests across the country. Among right-thinking and progressive lumber companies, there are few vestiges of the old cut-and-get-out policy anymore. Not as often either do you hear of preservation aims in terms of leaving every tree, limb, twig, and leaf as-is, no matter what, "untouched by human hands."

Over the years, man has discovered his impact on the earth, its flora and fauna, and has realized that things are not the same as they were before hordes of white men swarmed across the West in search of beaverskins and gold. Fortunately, unlike minerals, forests are renewable resources. If sound management is applied to them in time, the planet will not be denuded of its trees.

To this end, new and revolutionary forest theories and practices are being studied and developed in Whitaker's Forest, directed toward producing healthy growing trees, stable mountain slopes, a functioning watershed, clean streams, and a thriving fish and animal life.

The Big Trees, being a breed apart, require some special considerations different from those of most forests. The giants are, after all, one of the earth's natural wonders, remnants of a race born in antiquity, a cherished heritage to hold in trust for generations of the future—tremendous living things to which the world flocks in worshipful awe. Already well into old age, how much longer can they endure? One thing should be abundantly clear: there can be no more giants as we know them today unless there be a multitude of young replacements coming up in sites conducive to growth and survival. It follows then as the night the day, whatever should be done to insure Big Tree continuity must be done—by a public agency such as the Forest Service, by the lumber industry, by the public at large.

Mindful of our heritage, intense effort is being expended to preserve the giant trees the pioneers found grouped on the mountain benches overlooking their gold fields. Through the establishment of national forests and parks, through private subscription and public funds and unswerving dedication by conservation-minded individuals and organizations, the few remaining groves of Big Trees have been brought under supervision, to become, in a sense, a great outdoor museum. By the same token, it has also followed that they become popular recreation areas, some well developed for that purpose; each protected by heroic fire prevention measures.

Still, if you were to inspect letters and diaries of the Forty-Niners, you would discover cause for reflection.

You would read that the forest floor of those times was open and grassed and studded with wildflowers; animal life was plentiful. Small lightning-set fires occurred often, but major ones were rare because the scrubby underbrush was burned off before it could burgeon into mountainous forests of kindling. With the trash vegetation removed, mineral soil was exposed. Natural regeneration took place as seeds dropped and the sun drew sprouts upward into the first years of their lives. A new forest was on the way.

Today, especially within government preserves, much of the forest, long protected and therefore mostly untouched by fire, is a tall, impenetrable thicket, tinder-dry, whose mushrooming undergrowth has forced the wildlife out into clearings along meadow and stream. When a fire erupts in such an accumulation as this, it quickly becomes a holocaust of monstrous proportions that makes headlines sometimes for weeks and can eventually destroy some of the giants.

Under traditional fire-preventation and suppression programs, the Big Tree forests tend to remain clogged and choked except for the central areas, given over to roads, parking, and construction, lovingly trampled by millions of visitors each year, and consequently presenting still another problem.

Bearing all these aspects in mind, the staff at Whitaker's Forest has worked with numerous management practices to try and determine how to bring a Big Tree area into more normal ecology. By selective cutting and controlled burning, experimental plots have been cleared of their fuel trees and shrubs, and spared concentrated human erosion. Some companion trees—young pine, the white fir and incense cedar, vigorous competitors, have been removed, opening up the forest and releasing vital elements of space, sun, and nutrients to the Big Trees and sugar pines, in this way initiating in them a spurt of rapid growth.

Soon thereafter, with the renewal of grasses and flowers and young shoots—and at last, room to move around and find browse —wildlife once again flourishes, the deer, the bear, and smaller creatures, both predator and prey. Were this in an unrestricted area, people also would come. They, too, would enjoy the open park-like groves, where they can move about freely and view not just the crowns of the giants high above the depressing overmature thickets, but the enormous red trunks as well, all the way up from their gnarled bases.

In Whitaker's Forest, management guidelines are being developed that hopefully will promote future timber growth, healthy, vigorous, and scenic, and which will counteract some of man's well-intentioned but less desirable effects on his precious sequoias.

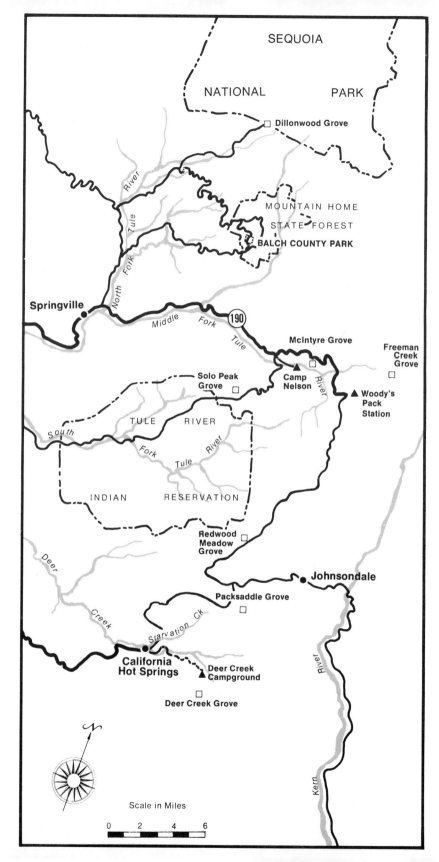

SEQUOIA

NATIONAL   PARK

□ Dillonwood Grove

MOUNTAIN HOME

STATE FOREST

BALCH COUNTY PARK

North Fork Tule River

Springville ●

Middle Fork Tule (190)

McIntyre Grove

Freeman Creek Grove □

▲ □ Camp Nelson

River

Solo Peak Grove □

▲ Woody's Pack Station

South Fork Tule River

TULE   RIVER

INDIAN   RESERVATION

Redwood Meadow Grove □

Johnsondale ●

Deer Creek

Packsaddle Grove □

Starvation Ck

California Hot Springs ●

▲ Deer Creek Campground

□ Deer Creek Grove

Kern River

N

Scale in Miles

0   2   4   6

Southern
Big Tree Country

South of Sequoia and Kings Canyon national parks, you will find a number of Big Tree groves in the Sequoia National Forest, a few easily accessible and interesting enough to make their exploration worthwhile. And then there are the many mature giants of Mountain Home State Forest and Balch County Park in Tulare County.

Mountain Home State Forest, a several-thousand acre preserve along the North Fork and the North Fork of the Tule River's Middle Fork, is a scientifically managed forest. Here you can see what happens when logged-over areas have been brought back. The slash and diseased timber has been cut and cleared, the fiercely competing white fir eliminated. Plantings of red fir and pine have been set out and some second-growth sequoias thinned to permit faster growth of the most promising trees. The result so far is that the remaining giants have flourished, providing visitors with unobstructed views of some very splendid sequoias.

The highway into the state forest leads to the best stands of Big Trees, where you will find excellent campsites among the giants. Some at Frazier Mill were born after milling operations ceased in 1886. Don't miss the small but picturesque Rosecrans Grove beside Hedrick Pond.

Summit Road winds on east of the central visitor area and leads to Shake Camp Campground and a pack station that provides horses for adventuring into the back country. On the Camp Lena Road, connecting Balch Park and Summit roads, you'll find a number of things to grab your attention. One is the Centennial Stump, what remains of one of the first sequoias cut for the astonishment of an unbelieving public.

The tree that once stood here was reported to have been 111 feet around and a good 300 feet tall—too magnificent to leave out there in the forest with no one to appreciate it! So in 1877 promoters had it cut 24 feet above the flaring base, where the diameter wasn't quite so awesome. Then they ordered the stump hollowed and cut into manageable slabs and later reassembled for display. Something evidently

*The Hercules Tree is today a curiosity but in days
gone by it has sometimes been a handy refuge.*

For Bucks Only

SUPPOSE YOU ARE CAMPING there and a deer has just eaten a bouquet of store-bought flowers off your picnic table. What kind of a deer was he anyway? Well, it depends on where you are. In the coast redwood forest, the thief would be a black-tailed deer. His tail is black on top and white underneath. Your Sierra camp would attract a larger animal—the handsome mule deer. His ears are long and his tail white with a black tip.

Maybe this fellow that ate your flowers so contentedly was a buck with a large rack of antlers. That's right—antlers, not horns. Horns are made of hardened skin and are hollow and permanent and

without covering. Antlers belong to the deer kind—for bucks only, made of honest-to-gosh bone, and shed every year. A buck spends his whole summer growing them.

During the months you are on vacation, he feels thoroughly ouchy. His antlers, developing rapidly from small rounded knobs, are soft and sensitive and full of blood vessels. They hurt and bleed profusely when bumped against a tree or rock, and break easily, too. Their covering of short, stiff hair—called velvet—offers little protection. So the buck moves into open brushy country where he won't keep hitting his antlers against things and where curious vacationers won't

---

went awry, because the intended exhibit made it only to valley settlements and finally as far as San Francisco.

You'll find a loop trail starting at Shake Camp that will lead you to the largest sequoia in Mountain Home, the Adam Tree, and on to (you guessed it) the Eve Tree, girdled and readied for felling at the turn of the century, but still standing. Of interest also will be the Methuselah Tree at the group campground near the forest headquarters. Its 96-foot base circumference is the greatest of any standing sequoia in Mountain Home State Forest.

Undoubtedly the most interesting tree along Shake Camp Road is the Hercules Tree. Between 1897 and 1902 it was hollowed out by a man who expected to make the giant his home. However, he had not counted on the sap dripping from the living wood inside, and he abandoned it. Later, in the early 1930's some campers were grateful for the drippy safety of that interior, whence they fled from the wrath of a windstorm that threatened to level every tree in the forest around them.

Within Mountain Home State Forest is **Balch County Park** with its 200 huge Big Trees, nicely developed picnic and camp areas, and

(continued from p. 155)
keep trying to grab them.

By summer's end the velvet is beginning to shrivel, causing the antlers to itch. The buck rubs them against trees and scratches them with his hind hooves. Although he appears to be fighting the brush, he's really only trying to rid himself of the dried-up velvet now hanging in shreds and festooning down over his face.

By the time the buck finally succeeds, his antlers are no longer soft and blunt. They have become hard and soft-pointed. All through the autumn he strops and polishes them against trees and boulders until they are as shiny and sharp as possible—all of this

for defense and in preparation for the November to February rutting—or mating—season battles with other bucks.

The first day of confrontation comes when he and his rivals crash head-on for the favors of the does. Sometimes then, antlers tangle. Locked together, the two animals could at last collapse and die of starvation, but usually one or the other gives up the fight and walks away, leaving the victor to claim the herd of does for his own.

At the end of the mating season, a buck's antlers fall off. Without his finery he is not nearly as cocky and certainly more vulnerable to enemies, so all spring

---

two mirror-like ponds for trout fishing. There are two unusual sequoias in the park well worth seeking out. One is a dead giant cut clear through in 1897 but still standing as erect as ever, and the other the exquisitely beautiful Lady Alice Tree.

Until snow flies and closes the access roads, visitors enjoy the self-guiding nature trail that starts at the park headquarters and loops through the park and on into Mountain Home State Forest, where they can observe the experiments in forest management going on there.

Backtrack a bit now almost to Springville and take State Highway 190 eastward to Camp Nelson and on to Belknap Campground, a fine place to base while exploring. All along the way on both sides of the Middle Fork's south fork from Camp Nelson to Wheel Meadows you will find quite an array of Big Trees. A trail runs the full length of McIntyre Grove.

Another grove—one that might challenge any desire to complete an inventory of ALL sequoia groves—is the **Solo Peak Grove** of a thousand or more giants that used to be known as the Black Mountain Grove. It is situated on a high divide between tributaries of the Middle

long he lies low, browsing quietly and peacefully. Until about May.

When that time comes, new knobs appear on the buck's head and once again he is quick with his hooves. With head held high, he struts through the forest and becomes more sociable.

Each summer his rack of antlers will branch until he has four or five on each side, depending upon whether any of them has been injured during development. This number he probably keeps during his years of full glory. With the approach of old age, however, he usually sports fewer and fewer points until, near the end of his life, he may be carrying the same kind of simple spikes he bore his very first year.

So there's no telling a buck's age by the number of points on his rack of antlers.

Always remembering to stand beyond the reach of his hooves, you can admire and take his picture, for his soft brown eyes are often deceiving. For no apparent reason he is prone to strike out with those knife-sharp hooves of his. But should you search a bit among the giant redwoods, you just could come upon a set of sun-bleached antlers to take home from your vacation—unless you prefer to leave them where they lie for the forest rodents to chew up in building their teeth for greater gnawing power.

---

and South forks of the Tule River. Excellent country for hikes, it can also be explored by car via dirt road from Camp Nelson or 40 miles of dirt from Porterville through the Tule Indian Reservation.

The several hundred big sequoias in **Freeman Creek Grove**, a mile from Highway 190 and east of Quaking Aspen Meadow, are truly splendid. Best to park at Woody's Pack Station if permission is granted, then hoof it along the trail that takes off from there into the Kern River watershed. With no roads intruding into this remote basin, it is a place where you can get away from it all. Be sure to leave the trail as it crosses Freeman Creek and ease your way eastward alongside the stream. South of it you will find the largest sequoias.

Driving along the pleasantly winding Western Divide Highway, a traveler suddenly leaves pine and fir and comes upon the mature Big Trees of **Redwood Meadow** beside the road. By taking off from there on foot, westerly, about a mile to Horse Meadow Creek, a peaceful hour or two or three can be whiled away just walking and looking at some really soaring red trunks.

To reach **Packsaddle Grove**, you would return to the Great Valley to the Porterville area, then proceed southeastward to Fountain

The Hollow Log in Balch County Park
attracts old and young alike.

Spring before once again heading some 20 miles up into the mountains to California Hot Springs and beyond to Pine Flat. From there, take the little dirt road leading north. Down below along Starvation Creek, you will see some Big Trees. The only way to enjoy them close up is to ease your way down into the steep ravine. Just take off from one of the signs reading "Type I redwood grove" posted on roadside trees.

Southernmost of all Big Tree groves is **Deer Creek**. From Pine Flat follow the dirt road that goes east three miles to the Deer Creek Mill Campground. Get out there and look up. On the slope you will see the vanguard of a larger grove about 40 minutes hike from the campground parking area.

If it's a workout you'd like at this point, you can tackle what remains of an old logging skid road. If the prospect intimidates you, take the slightly longer but much easier path that takes off to the right of the steep skid road. Either way, the stand of young sequoias followed by several dozen impressive red giants should add greatly to anyone's store of cherished explorations and adventures.

Index